The Cost of Living Crisis

Time to End Economic Injustice

Michael Calderbank

First published as a paper back in Great Britain in February 2015
By Comerford and Miller
Under their A Radical Read Imprint
36 Grosvenor Road
West Wickham
BR4 9PY

http://www.radicalread.com

info@radicalread.co.uk

ISBN 978-1-871204-29-2

Printed and Bound in the UK by SRP Exeter

Cover design Howard Lester howardlester@btinternet.com
Typeset Robbie Griffiths

Contents

Dr Michael Calderbank lives in London, where he works in Parliament as a researcher for trade unions. He is Co-Editor of the lively and influential left magazine *Red Pepper*. Michael describes himself as a community activist, campaigning against cuts to public services, privatisation and attacks on the welfare state.

Acknowledgements

This book emerged out of research I was commissioned to undertake for the Trade Union Coordinating Group, which comprises nine national trade unions (BFAWU, FBU, NAPO, NUJ, NUT, PCS, POA, RMT, and URTU) to co-ordinate campaigning activities in Parliament and beyond. I am indebted to all the TUCG unions for their support.

I'm particularly grateful to Simeon Andrews for encouraging me to tackle the subject of privatisation in a booklet I wrote in 2013, and then taking forward research on "The Great Pay Robbery" and "The Cost of Living Crisis", much of which forms the basis of the present work. I'd also like to thank Mark Serwotka and Mick Cash for kindly agreeing to publish forewords in the respective booklets and Michelle Stanistreet, Sarah Kavanagh and Frances Rafferty at the NUJ, James Croy and Dan Crimes at the RMT, and Andrew Fisher at PCS for reading over earlier drafts. Special thanks go to Tom Walker for his work in knocking the original text into shape in remarkably short order. The responsibility for any errors or omissions which remain is all mine.

I'd also like to thank Russell Miller and Ted Knight for all their help in editing and publishing the present volume, and for putting up with the delays caused by my time spent on *Red Pepper* magazine and helping out with the Labour Representation Committee. I'd like to thank all my comrades there, particularly Hilary Wainwright and John McDonnell, for their support and sheer political drive.

And last but not least I'd like to thank Elaine and John Calderbank, my Mum and Dad, for a million and one things, not least their willingness to proof-read at short notice!

Foreword

In the last few years we have come to learn a new phrase, the 'cost of living crisis'. It reflects the fact that people's incomes in this country have been decimated (literally, in the sense of being cut by 10%). This is unprecedented. People's incomes in the UK have not suffered such a sustained decline for more than a century.

Some of the quarter of a million public sector workers I represent are up to 20% worse off in real terms due to the combined impacts of pay freezes, pay caps and higher pension contributions.

For many workers the effects have been worse: losing work entirely or losing secure reasonably paid employment for the insecurity of low pay temporary or zero hours contracts.

This cost of living crisis is presented as inevitable: the economy crashed and "we're all in together", said David Cameron. But we haven't been. The rich have got richer while the poor have got poorer. The super-rich have done exceedingly well and big business has seen its taxes slashed by 25% – and that's if they pay them.

In the last year, when George Osborne was proclaiming his marvellous though much-delayed recovery, the economic data from the government told us that only households in the top 20% were better off, the other 80% got poorer still – during a 'recovery'.

The reality is we have an economy structured to funnel money from the many to the few at the top. That has only intensified since the crash as the poorest have been made to pay with their jobs, pay and public services.

This book documents the cost of living crisis, but more importantly signposts a way out of the economic injustice that is damaging people's lives. The job for those in the trade union movement, and beyond, is to use this analysis to mobilise for action to end that injustice.

Mark Serwotka
General Secretary of the Public and Commercial Services Union

1

The Great Leap Backwards

Inevitably, those worst effected by recessions are those with low incomes. But the depth of the poverty and debt into which a section of the British population was driven following the 2008 financial crash and its immediate aftermath has been without parallel in post-war records. That such destitution could be seen on the streets of one of the world's most advanced economies in the 21st Century was sufficiently shocking to draw fierce condemnations from the normally reserved ranks of faith leaders, charities and care professionals.

Yet what distinguishes this latest recession is that just about every class been hit, bar the obscenely rich – who have done pretty well. Unless there are significant changes to the structure of the economy, worry over the cost of essential goods and services will continue to be with the majority of us for the foreseeable future.

Of course, we can expect Chancellors to periodically announce things are improving. "There are more jobs in the economy than ever before", but only because people are having to hold down 2 or even more low paid jobs just to pay their way, and are having to continue working late in life because they cannot afford to retire. Yet if the figures show that the economy is enjoying a measure of recovery, people are entitled to ask "*who* is enjoying the benefits of this return to growth?"

After the deepest, most prolonged recession since modern records began over half a century ago,[1] the British economy began to recover, despite the needless delay brought on by the strangulating effect of austerity measures. However, not until the middle of 2014 did the economy reach its level before the 2008 financial crisis hit, having seen gross domestic product (GDP) hit by 7.2%[2] and official unemployment figures reaching 2.7 million at the depth of the recession.[3]

Notwithstanding the best efforts of David Cameron and George Osborne to talk up their economic "success", the modest recovery failed to generate much of a feel-good factor. They should not have been surprised. We feel good when we enjoy a rising standard of living and an improving quality of life. This has just not been happening. Even the Bank of England governor Mark Carney warned that the modest recovery was vulnerable, claiming that the government caused inflation through policies like the "Help to Buy" scheme that was responsible for the housing bubble. In any case, trends in the headline rate of GDP are not much consolation to families who find that they are priced out of home ownership and forced to live as part of "Generation Rent". Neither does it do anything to justify the vast disparities of wealth that exist in our society, in which the assets of the richest 1% exceed that of the poorest 55% of the population.[4]

At the same time, the Trussell Trust charity, which provides emergency food aid, reported a 163% increase in use of its food banks as financial hardship leaves families across the country unable even to afford such basics. Given the extent of shame that exists over accepting charitable help, reports of people who manage to feed themselves only by cutting out other essentials like heating costs or taking out costly payday loans, and the numbers in areas when no food bank currently operates, the real extent of food poverty is likely to be larger still. As we shall see, attacks on welfare benefit entitlements and the introduction of draconian "sanctions" have had a particularly dramatic impact on the incomes of the poorest in society.

The falling wage share

But it is not just a minority of those facing the greatest hardship who have experienced a general squeeze in their living standards. Most earners outside the super-rich have suffered as the percentage of total national income going to wages has been eroding since the early 1980s. This occurred as a result of neoliberal policies such as the attacks on trade unions, devastation of manufacturing industry and the rise of low-paid service sector jobs as an increasingly casualization of the labour market enabled greater exploitation. As TUC research has shown:

... between 1960 and 1980 the share of wages in national income fluctuated between around 58 and 61 percent (apart from a brief upward spike in the mid-1970s) but declined sharply in the early 1980s and has been below 56 percent since 1982, falling as low as 51 percent in the late 1990s. Meanwhile, the profit share (operating surpluses as a percentage of national income) rose from 24 percent in 1980 to 28 percent in 2011. The decoupling of earnings from output is not a phenomenon unique to the UK but has occurred in a majority of rich nations, although to varying degrees.

At the same time that the wage share has been falling, the UK dispersion of earnings has been widening, with real full time earnings at the 90th percentile doubling between 1978 and 2008 compared with growth of only 25 percent at the 10th percentile (and no growth at all in the bottom half of the earnings distribution since 2003). Overall, our research finds that the falling wage share accounts for about a third of the decline in median wages relative to GDP in the UK over the last 35 years, with the other two-thirds being accounted for by increased dispersion of earnings.[5]

Overall, the experience of successive governments – first under the Thatcherite Tories and then New Labour – has been that a growing gulf has emerged between the rate of growth in the economy and the increase in workers' wages.

Which priority? Cost of living – or pleasing the markets

Ed Miliband's talk of a "cost of living crisis" touched on a real sense that millions of people, as they find it more difficult to make ends meet, feel that the economy is run for the benefit of a tiny few at the top. The instance he began to focus on – the greed of the Big Six energy firms making billions in profit, whilst bills have continued to rocket – is by no means an exceptional case of how our economy is structured to the detriment of ordinary working people. That said, Miliband's 'remedy' of a two year price freeze, though not unwelcomed, did not address the systemic nature of the problem. The energy bosses can pre-empt the measure, with front-loaded price freezes, or by cutting investment in the energy industry to ride out the temporary cap on prices, thus continuing to protect their profits, at the consumer's expense.

Across the board, a similar timidity has been in evidence, most notably perhaps in the failure of the Labour Party to commit to taking rail back into public ownership. But the problem is not only that these measures are insufficiently robust, but also that Labour approached the 2015 General Election committed to the same fiscal straitjacket of austerity that the Tories had already announced for 2015-16.

In its desperation to appear "credible" to the City markets, Ed Balls accepted a framework that runs contrary to the kind of spending priorities government would pursue if it was genuinely making action on the "cost of living" its main priority. How does it help struggling public sector workers to give them a real terms pay cut? How is it desirable to leave the travelling public at the mercy of a privatised rail system, that has seen prices rise three times faster than wages?[6] Or to cap overall welfare spending, irrespective of the levels of need, while doing little to stop the lavish subsidy to landlords via spiralling Housing Benefit costs?

Pension rip-off

If Labour was to do more than pay lip-service to tackling the cost of living crisis which it rightly diagnoses, it would need to reverse the damaging attacks on pension arrangements introduced by the coalition parties. A policy which mean people have been left having to work longer, pay more and get less back at the end of their working lives. The switch from the Retail Price Index (RPI) measure of inflation to the lower Consumer Price Index (CPI) – which does not include housing costs – will mean, for example, that a lecturer in further education with a £10,000 pension would lose around £36,000 or more over the average (25 year) course of retirement, while university lecturers with an £18,000 pension would lose out by a colossal £65,000 over their retirement.[7]

The cost of the increase in the pensionable age is not just felt in financial terms; there is the quality of life factor, which is destroyed by the extra years taken from a worker's retirement. At an age when years of toil should be rewarded with a leisurely dignified retirement, the elderly are now expected to still be slogging away at work. Yet those working are the lucky ones. There are barriers for older workers seeking work. The years when they should be enjoying retirement could well be years spent on the dole and facing "sanctions" for not trying hard enough. In the case of the fire and rescue service, the change to the pension age will mean that firefighters will be expected to work until they are 60, in a job that demands high levels of fitness and physical duress that make the work unsuitable, and potentially unsafe, for people in their later years – not to mention the endangered public.

The cuts are worsening existing inequalities. Take the impact on women: since nearly 40% of women's jobs are in the public sector (compared to 15% of men's), women have felt disproportionately the effect of job losses and privatisation following cuts to public spending. But the coalition's attacks on pensions mean that even if hard-pressed workers such as carers and teaching assistants manage to keep their jobs, they will still be faced by a double-whammy of increasing pension contributions and reduced final pay-outs. The government was talking about public sector workers enjoying "gold-plated" pensions at a time when the average (mean) pension of a male local government worker was £4,200 a year, whilst women's pensions were worth an average of just £2,800.[8]

This is because women are more likely to face age discrimination, to be employed in lower-paid areas of work in the public sector and to work part-time hours, perhaps because they are juggling a career with unpaid caring responsibilities. Women are more likely to feel the impact of cuts to social services provided by local authorities, as essential forms of support are withdrawn. Women are also more likely to receive tax credits and welfare benefits to support low incomes, so they have been particularly badly hit by the coalition attacks on welfare payments. But where is the party that will offer to reverse the attacks on our pensions, to scrap the cuts to local government and to defend social security entitlements to guarantee a basic minimum standard of living? What is needed is not just a strategy to limit further growth in inequalities, but to radically reverse this process.

Incomes hammered by the crisis

The pressure on incomes has been made all the more intense after the cost of essential goods and services, and particularly the cost of housing, is taken into consideration. Levels of housebuilding are running at less than half the 250,000 to 300,000 that experts calculate are needed to stand still, while the number of "affordable" homes (properties let at 80% of the market rent, in reality way beyond what is genuinely affordable for many) fell by as much as 26% last year to an eight-year low.[9]

The escalation in house prices has made home ownership unaffordable to a substantial section of society, with generations now trapped into a private rented sector plagued by insecurity of tenure, overcrowding and poor conditions. Already housing charity Shelter reports that the number of people struggling to pay their rent or mortgage each month has increased by 44% over the past year to 7.8 million, while almost one in three adults (around 15 million people) say housing costs are causing stress and depression in their family.[10]

But if the pressure is telling today, the crisis in housing is only likely to intensify. Analysts forecast that house prices could rocket up by 35% by 2020 and rents are projected to soar by 39% over the same period.[11] Meanwhile many homeowners who have stretched their finances to take out a mortgage in conditions where interest rates are low could easily find themselves over-exposed as rates are likely to rise. Using OBR figures, the Resolution Foundation has calculated that an increase in interest rates of 5% by 2018 would put 2 million households at risk of having their homes repossessed, with half of these being families with children.[12]

In this book we will see that the squeeze on household incomes has been compounded by the rising costs of many other essential everyday items of expenditure. Like childcare fees, transport costs, energy and telephone bills. These costs have led to a significant part of the population finding they have been unable to make ends meet from month to month. A new market has emerged for exploitation by predatory "payday loan" companies, charging extravagant rates of interest and trapping people in worsening spirals of rolled-over debts. The cost of meeting loan repayments or credit card charges is itself a key part of the cost of living for millions of households.

In reality although the official rate of inflation (measured by the Consumer Prices Index or CPI) has been running at around 1.5%, this fails to take into the fact that low income households are forced to spend a greater proportion on essential goods and services, which have been rising at a faster than average pace, than are the rich. The New Economics Foundation's Real Britain Index (RBI) measures the differences between the effective rate of inflation paid by households across the income distribution scale and the official CPI measure of inflation:

> For the period as a whole, from January 2006, our RBI suggests that prices paid by the poorest 10% have risen by nearly 32%. For comparison, the official CPI measure suggests a price increase of just 20%. For the rich, meanwhile, prices have risen by 27%. From poorest to richest, the overall pattern is clear: the better-off you are the less impact inflation has had... To give some sense of what these figures mean, a typical civil servant, earning the median pay for the civil service of £24,000, would face an RBI inflation rate of 2.36% (in July 2014). A typical nurse, again earning the median pay, faced an inflation of 2.37%. The headline, CPI, rate of inflation at that stage was 1.6%; it can be seen immediately that, for example, pegging pay awards to CPI would result in a loss of real earnings for both these two.[13]

This shows that the poorest families are disproportionately hit by the effect of the rising cost of everyday essentials like food and heating.

But why has the cost of so many of the basic goods and services we need in our daily lives been rising so steeply? What unites much of the material considered in this book is the effect of privatising and/or slashing back public services in favour of private sector providers. Their first priority is to deliver dividends for their shareholders rather than prioritise value and quality for customers. Far from emboldening risk-taking "entrepreneurs" to innovate, private companies have often played a parasitical role, sucking up public subsidy, capitalising on state-led research and development, or exploiting elements of a monopoly to make vast profits off our backs. A combination of the inherent inefficiencies of fragmenting services to allow for competition, weak regulators intimidated by powerful corporate interests and a political class willing to reward failure has created dysfunctional markets run to make private profits where there once existed public services run for the public good.

The austerity-driven politics of slashing spending on public services is not motivated by economic inevitability, but political choice. The more services are no longer funded by taxes, the more markets will exist to sell them as private commodities to those who can afford to pay. Rather than ensuring that our resources are shared fairly so that a basic quality of life is guaranteed for all, the market-driven world is one where sick, disabled, elderly, or unemployed people who cannot afford to pay the price are left to rot, just so long as shareholders can profit from running services for those who can.

On top of the war on welfare benefits, public spending has been slashed since 2010, with severe reductions in local council budgets meaning services have been cut to the bone or abandoned altogether: social care for elderly and disabled people, SureStart centres, libraries, breakfast and after-school clubs, leisure centres... the list goes on and on. But according to the Office of Budget Responsibility, the coalition will only have implemented 40% of the cuts it has announced by May 2015, with the remaining 60% cuts running through to 2019.

The result will be that state spending will be slashed back to just 35% of Gross Domestic Product, a level not seen in Britain since the 1930s.[14] With Labour already pledged to stick within George Osborne's plans for the first two years, it is clear that the overall thrust of austerity will continue regardless of the outcome of the general election.

Basic contradictions

So while Ed Miliband's pre-election promise to address the cost of living crisis as a priority looked good; he also committed his Party to austerity, undermining his own case. How does it help workers in the public sector struggling to cope with the cost of living to deliver a pay freeze, or in other words, a real terms cut to their pay? How does it help a young couple struggling to meet the costs of bringing up a family to find the value of their child benefit is to fall? You do not have to be a genius to spot a fundamental problem here.

At the same time, a government that was genuinely committed to helping to lift the burden of the cost of living could win broad popular support. Labour enjoyed a noticeable bounce in the polls following the announcement of an energy price freeze, with voters distinctly unimpressed by the blackmail from fat cat energy bosses threatening to turn off the lights. In fact, a YouGov survey showed voters were prepared to go much further, with 68% saying the energy companies should be in the public sector and just 21% believing they should remain privately owned.[15] Similarly the halfway-house proposal advocated by the Labour Party, to let the public sector compete with private companies, when franchises expire, falls short of reintegrating the whole rail system under public ownership. A policy decision made despite the overwhelming public support for this measure shown consistently in polls.[16]

This book examines the structural factors and political choices behind the cost of living crisis. In "The change we need" section at the end of each chapter, it advances the kind of policies that a government would pursue if it made tackling the cost of living crisis its over-riding priority and rejected the austerity measures demanded by big financial and corporate interests. This would mean having conviction in the value of public services, and rejecting the failed model of privatised services run for the benefit of a tiny minority.

2

Pay

Rich get richer – at our expense

As the Coalition government neared the end of its term pay became a major political issue. Working people across the country began mobilising behind the demand that "Britain needs a pay rise". True, a tiny handful have been considerably less in need than others, since the average pay of a FTSE 100 company boss stood at £4.3million in 2014, which even on conservative estimates works out at well over £1,000 per hour.[1]

As newspaper headlines told hard-pressed workers in their first week back at work in 2014, it would only take these fatcat bosses until Wednesday lunchtime to pocket what it will take the average worker the whole of 2014 to earn. Are these rewards for success? Hardly – failed Tesco Chief Executive Philip Clarke, who was on a £1.1 million salary, got a £10 million pay off when he was ousted by the Board for failing to turn around the company's performance, and the company agreed to pay his whopping basic pay for a whole 12 months after his departure. On top of which he'd amassed a £11.5million pension pot.[2] Meanwhile the average supermarket cashier was earning just £6.73 per hour,[3] significantly lower than the Living Wage which stood at £7.85 (or £9.15 an hour in London) in 2014.[4] Perhaps politicians are still "intensely relaxed" about people getting filthy rich, but it is harder to be quite so understanding if you can't even afford to put food on the table for your kids when you get home.

As Cameron and Clegg prepared to face the electorate, the UK stood as the fifth most unequal of the leading 27 economies in the OECD. As the Low Pay Commission argued:

> This growing inequality is represented by a growing disparity between rewards at the top of the income distribution to low pay at the bottom. While the number of people being below the Living Wage continues to rise, figures from the High Pay Centre show that the share of national income going to the top 1 per cent of the income distribution has more than doubled since 1979 from 6% to 14%.[5]

Analysts[6] have observed a growing trend towards a polarisation of the workforce during the 1980s and 90s, in which:

> ... the highest earners moved away from the middle earners and those in the middle moved away in turn from those at the bottom, meaning that increasing numbers of workers found themselves falling below the relative low pay threshold defined here as two thirds of gross hourly median pay among all employees. From a low of just 15 per cent of employees in 1975, the proportion of low paid workers peaked at 23 per cent in 1996. Since then the proportion has changed very little.[7]

This polarisation further accelerated in the wake of the 2008 financial crisis, during which unemployment was to an extent mitigated by the creation of low-paying, temporary and/or part-time jobs in those sectors with the highest concentration of low-skilled work. By 2014, there were 5.24 million workers in Britain paid below the living wage, the independently-set figure which represents the minimum amount needed to enjoy a basic, but socially acceptable standard of living.[8] This represented an increase of 420,000 on the previous 12 months alone.[9]

Falling real wages

But low paid workers have not been alone in having lost out over recent decades. Our pay packets took a real hit following the financial crisis, but this has itself to be seen in the context of a longer-term decline in the growth of real wages, also affecting middle income earners. It would be wrong to see the crisis as the sole cause for the squeeze on our pay. As the Office for National Statistics has shown:

> Annual real wage growth averaged 2.9% in the 1970s and 1980s, then roughly halved to 1.5% in the 1990s. The rate slowed again to an average of 1.2% in the 2000s.[10]

So long before the banks ran into trouble, the share of value produced in the economy going to labour was being squeezed, with a growing 'decoupling' of rates of real wage growth from growth in GDP throughout the first decade of the new millennium. Amongst other things, this reflects the marketisation of the economy, the shift from manufacturing towards a service-based economy, and the relative weakness of the power of the trade unions.

But if growth in wages had been sluggish even beforehand, since 2009-10 nominal wages have failed to keep pace with the rate of price inflation, meaning real wages have been falling for the longest sustained period since at least 1964 and contributed to average incomes in 2011-12 (adjusting for inflation) being lower than in 2002-3[11]:

> ... real wages fell by 2.2% per annum between Q1 2010 and Q2 2013 ... the recent episode is the longest sustained period of falling real wages in the UK on record.[12]

Even using the lower CPI measure of inflation, real hourly wages have fallen on average by 8.5% since 2009, wiping out totally the slow progress made earlier in the decade.[13] The Resolution Foundation has spoken of recent trends as representing "an unparalleled collapse in real wages":

> In the most accurate large-scale survey data, the median wage of UK employees was £23,800 in 2007-8. Five years later, it was £21,900, a fall of 7.8%. A drop of wages in this magnitude has not been seen before, including in recessions...[14]

Even with a return to economic growth, the value of real wages has continued to fall until well in 2014. By 2015 we might finally see the real value of wages finally start to recover, but it remains to be seen if to what extent the recovery can sustain and gather momentum. Even the Office for Budget Responsibility was forecasting that we would not get back to the level of 2002 earnings until 2018-19, whilst analysts PwC argue that we will need to wait until around 2020.[15] For the last decade and a half, the same hard day at work had seen the pay packet most of us take home being worth less and less.

Casualisation – low paid, part-time jobs

Economists have argued that relative to the contraction of the economy, the experience of previous recessions might have led us to expect unemployment to have been even deeper and more prolonged than the UK has in fact experienced this time – but that, conversely, we would have expected to have seen a more rapid recovery in the level of real wages once the economy returned to growth. In effect, we have seen a trade-off where increasing 'labour market flexibility' – the creation of more casualised, low-paid, temporary and/or part-time jobs – has to an extent moved into the gap left as full-time jobs have been destroyed, at the cost of a squeeze on pay. Partly as a result of punitive welfare reforms which force people off benefits into poorly paying work, we began to witness a major spike in "in-work" poverty:

> For the first time, there are now more people in working poverty than in out-of-work poverty. 6.7 million of the 13 million people in poverty in the UK are in a family where someone works. That is 52% of the total.[16]

Particularly concerning is the prospect that the austerity-driven reshaping of the labour market was not a temporary fix whilst the economy recovered but is continuing to limit the share of GDP taken in wages, meaning that economic recovery alone would not necessarily be sufficient to lift people out of poverty. Instead, the trend towards casualisation of work can be seen in a number of recent developments. By 2014, for example, 4.3 million workers were now officially registered as "self-employed", a rise of 15% since 2009-10. This is thought to have "compensated" for around 40% of job losses since the crash, without which unemployment would have topped 3 million.[17]

Bogus self-employment, zero hour's contracts

Does this substantial rise in "self-employment" mean there had been an uptake of entrepreneurialism by British workers, suddenly confident enough to launch their own businesses? Far from it; rather, the shift towards self-employment status was more a case of bosses offloading their employment overheads (employers' National Insurance contributions, but also maternity pay, sick pay, holiday pay, pension contributions, and redundancy pay) onto the workers themselves, often also putting their working hours on a more "flexible" basis.

The trend towards self-employment was related to the use of payroll companies, which had become widespread throughout industries like construction and rail engineering. Here, even if the worker continued to work for a single company, they could be transferred from pay-as-you-earn (PAYE) status and employed instead on a contract stating they are self-employed, losing their rights as an employee, with a fee being deducted directly from their wages by the payroll company for its services. (Alternatively, the employer might operate an "umbrella company" allowing them to claim back tax relief on the PAYE workers' expenses in order to offset their National Insurance liabilities – a legal tax dodge.) Workers in these industries are frequently offered a more attractive nominal hourly rate of pay, which after deductions looks distinctly less so. In an example cited by the RMT, a nominal rate of £9.50 an hour was translated after deductions into a rate of £6.19, coincidentally the then adult rate of the national minimum wage.[18] In addition to the dramatic effect on the pay and job security of the workforce, this practice is estimated to cost the taxpayer in excess of £1.9 billion every year.[19]

Workers designated "self-employed" but working for one or more companies via payroll companies or employment agencies have frequently been employed on a "zero hours" basis, where they do not know how many hours of work will be available from one week to the next. This can put workers in a very precarious and uncertain situation, making it difficult to plan ahead – both financially and more generally. The prospect of having hours suddenly withdrawn without notice is also used as a disciplinary tool by management, as well as to prevent workers from claiming entitlements such as rest breaks or challenging unsafe working conditions.

Government statistics showed that 583,000 people were thought to be on zero-hours contracts (1.9% of the workforce) – double the figure at the end of 2012. But this is widely thought to underestimate the extent of their use, with the Chartered Institute of Personnel and Development estimating just over one million workers (3.1%) were on such contracts in 2013.[20]

Not all workers on zero hours contracts are designated self-employed, and some might have been bound by an "exclusivity clause" to work for just one company, even though it makes no commitment to making hours available – a situation on which even the Coalition government accepted it needs to clamp down. Nearly half (48%) of employers in the hotels, catering and leisure industry admitting to using the contracts, but this is not just a feature of private sector employment, since many public and voluntary sector workers are also working on them. A third (35%) of education employers and more than a quarter (27%) of health care employers report using zero hours contracts.[21] 99 out of 131 NHS hospital trusts (75%) responding to a Freedom of Information request confirmed they used such contracts. Adult social care workers are frequently employed on such a basis, and where they are not paid for travelling time between visits can end up working for less than minimum wage.

The rising use of zero hours has clearly begun to have a chilling effect on earnings, as evidence presented to the Scottish Affairs Select Committee inquiry demonstrates: "20% of workers on zero hours contracts are paid less than their permanent equivalents doing the same job, 5% are paid less than the national minimum wage and 6% turn up for work to find none available."[22]

Holding down multiple jobs

Although official unemployment figures eventually started to decline in the second half of the Coalition's term , this conceals the fact that millions have been have been responding to job losses and falling real wages by taking multiple low-paid or temporary jobs in order to compensate. The widespread use of zero hours contracts has been part of a wider epidemic of "under-employment", where workers are unable to find enough hours to maintain their earnings.

Economists David Bell and David Blanchflower, in a study for the National Institute of Economic and Social Research, crunched the data and discovered that underemployment has risen from 6.2% in 2008 to 9.9% in 2012, with the impact especially noticeable among young workers.[23] With this degree of slack in the labour market, they consider that "even a substantial increase in aggregate demand is unlikely to exert significant upward pressure on real wages."[24]

Unpaid internships

When youth unemployment hits 20% and employers prefer experienced candidates it is understandable that young people have been willing to take up unpaid internships in order to get a foot in the door. Rather than providing properly structured and paid programmes of work experience, employers have all too often been prepared to exploit the non-payment of young people by requiring them to perform duties which would otherwise be fulfilled by paid staff.

It has been illegal for private employers to use unpaid interns as though they were employees, meaning that they should not be required to work set hours or fulfil the same responsibilities for an extended period (though this does not apply to charities, voluntary organisations or statutory bodies, which are entitled to take on interns on a "volunteer" basis[25]). However, unpaid internships have still been widely advertised, and their exploitation remained rife across industries like journalism, fashion design and politics. Parliament was told of one example where a young woman was working as an unpaid intern for a leading designer fashion-house:

She worked for 12 hours a day, sewing sequins on couture gowns that retailed for £5,000. I asked her what her terms and conditions were. She did not receive a penny in payment. She said, "We very often get pizza and occasionally we get shouted at."[26]

Sometimes young people will take on multiple unpaid internships without ever getting taken on as a paid employee. But where industries have become practically off-limits to those who have not first served as an intern, the practice is effectively restricting opportunities to those from relatively affluent families who can support young people living for weeks or months in London without any earnings. People who do not live in or near London are at a particular disadvantage given the exorbitant housing costs in the capital.

Such internships began to have a very damaging effect on employment and pay rates in the industries where they are commonplace, since employers have no incentive to create properly paid positions where there is a ready army of free labour to exploit. Thankfully as a result of campaigns by unions like the NUJ and campaign groups like Intern Aware we have started to see the courts force some employers to repay wages they had illegally withheld from their interns. But many more interns are understandably reluctant to deter possible employers by taking such action.

Workfare – modern slavery

If there is a "voluntary" element to the exploitation of unpaid interns, this cannot be said of the use of workfare schemes. This is where employers – including highly profitable companies like Marks and Spencer, McDonald's and Hilton Hotels, together with charities like Barnardo's and even some public sector bodies

– put benefit claimants to work unpaid, with the threat of their benefits being taken away if they fail to comply. The scheme builds on "reforms" introduced by James Purnell under Gordon Brown's government on the advice of David (later Lord) Freud, who now sits as a Tory peer and is a minister serving under Iain Duncan Smith. These allowed benefits to be withheld from jobseekers not deemed to be sufficiently active in looking to find work. The coalition then introduced Mandatory Work Activity, along with so-called Community Work Placements, which went one stage further and coerced benefit claimants into working for nothing.

Being coerced to work unpaid with the threat of being refused all means of subsistence is a modern form of slavery. The Slough office of the subsequently-discredited Work Programme provider A4e was marketing "free workers" to Primark, capable of filling "20-hour jobs".[27] On top of the exploitation of the benefit claimants themselves, it is also often bad for the pay and conditions of the existing paid workforce. Workers at Holland and Barrett have reportedly found that, since the introduction of workfare, the availability of much-needed overtime has disappeared.[28]

Similarly, Bakers' Union (BFAWU) members at Tangerine Confectionery were threatened with over two hundred compulsory redundancies from the company's Blackpool site. However, bosses were also explaining to managers that as suppliers to Marks and Spencer, they were required to take on unpaid benefit claimants on workfare schemes as 2% of the total company workforce. This example of "job-substitution" could be just the tip of the iceberg.

Low pay epidemic

Zero hours contracts, workfare and unpaid internships are part and parcel of the growing casualisation that has been levelling down pay and conditions across the board. The extent of poverty pay is absolutely shameful for an advanced economy and one of the richest countries on the planet. Last year official statistics showed that over 200,000 adults over 21 years of age were paid less than the national minimum wage of £6.31 an hour.[29] In addition, they say that is "almost certainly under reporting of unlawful non-payment".[30] This is especially likely to be true of incidents relating to migrant workers working in industries not covered by the Gangmasters' Licensing Authority. The exact mix of those falling under legal exemptions (for example where workers are provided accommodation owned by the employer) and illegal non-compliance is not known, although the Low Pay Commission believes that most fall under the latter heading.[31] Yet the rate of successful prosecutions of employers for non-compliance remains extraordinarily low.

In an answer to a written question tabled by Labour MP Karl Turner; Vince Cable revealed that by 2014 only two employers had been successfully prosecuted for illegal non-payment of the minimum wage – since 2010![32] Given that the coalition also axed thousands of civil servants' jobs at HMRC – the body responsible for enforcement of the minimum wage – the government can hardly shift the blame to over-stretched tax officials. Meanwhile employers like Condor Ferries exploit legal loopholes to pay seafarers from outside the European Economic Area as little as £2.32 per hour on vessels working out of British ports, pressuring rival companies like Stena Line to look at sacking their British workers and implementing a "non-UK crewing model" to compete.

But to the extent that better enforcement and tighter framing of minimum wage legislation would clear up such cases, the problem – though especially acute for those affected – is small in relation to the epidemic problem of legal low pay. The Low Pay Commission's 2014 report shows that 1.3 million workers (5.1%) in the UK worked in jobs that pay no more than the national minimum wage, which in early 2014 had been set at £6.31 an hour (over 21), £5.03 (18-20), £3.72 (16-17) and £2.68 (apprentice). Since its introduction in 1997 at a level most regard as excessively cautious (£3.60) it has risen slightly above average earnings, ahead of inflation, but behind the general growth in the economy (measured by nominal GDP).[33] However, since 2010 the real value of the minimum wage has fallen sharply. In October 2013, when taking into account RPI inflation, the adult minimum wage was "lower in real terms than at any point since 2003".[34] In October 2014 the minimum wage was increased to £6.50 an hour but this was from a historically low base.

Since the living wage – which, remember, is the *minimum* judged to afford workers a basic but socially acceptable standard of living – is presently set at £7.65 (or £8.80 in London, given the greater cost of living) and will increase later in the year, it is evident that compliance with the statutory minimum does not mean that employers are beginning to discharge their duty to pay workers enough to get by. Indeed, the fact that 5.24 million workers are paid an hourly rate which is insufficient to provide even the most basic standard of living is an outrage.

However, while it has become an important political reference point for campaigning against poverty pay, the living wage should not be taken in isolation as though achieving it were a panacea for all ills. Getting public sector bodies to commit to paying their staff a minimum wage, while welcome, is undermined if they do not make this a precondition for procuring services that have been outsourced to the private sector. Similarly, moral appeals to the conscience of employers are clearly inadequate. Even where the living wage is granted it would not automatically lift people out of poverty. The Resolution Foundation's *Low Pay Britain* report finds that even those paid the living wage fall under the threshold they set for low pay, based on hourly wages below two-thirds of gross median hourly pay for all employees.[35]

Poverty trap

It could be argued that the existence of low paid jobs in the economy was not in itself so bad so long as people take up opportunities to move on to better paid jobs later on. But economists and politicians also fear the impact of mass youth unemployment across the EU following the financial crash will have a prolonged scarring effect on the lifetime's earnings of a whole generation of young people.[36] Evidence also suggests that levels of social mobility and pay progression have often been very limited, with people getting stuck on a permanent treadmill of low-paying work throughout their working lives. One study found:

> Almost three-quarters (73%) of those who were low paid in 2002 remained on low pay in 2012 [while] more than two-in-five (44%) of all low paid employees over 25 have been stuck on low pay for the previous decade; half (51%) of those trapped on how pay are between the ages of 41-60. These are people who at the start of the previous decade, in 2002, were in the peak earning years of their lives (31-50) but who, despite this, were unable to progress out of low pay. This is particularly worrying because many, having already been stuck on low pay for a decade, have now reached an age where they will have limited scope for any subsequent pay progression throughout their careers.[37]

Of the study's cohort of low paid workers in 2002, 27% had remained stuck on low pay throughout the decade, and a further 46% found themselves back on low pay after having worked at least a year in a job paying over the low pay threshold in the interim. Less than a fifth (18%) had now managed to escape low paid work on a sustainable basis. The existence of such a low pay trap only serves to highlight the lasting dangers of the post-crash casualisation of the labour market for the future pay trajectory of the millions currently in low paid jobs in the absence of radical policy alternatives.

Deliberate political choices

Unless the effects of the post-crisis reshaping of the jobs market can be reversed, we will see continued exploitation of workers while the bosses walk away with the biggest share of the profits of growth. This is no accident. As Whittaker and Hurrell comment in their Resolution Foundation report:

> We might also point to a range of public policy choices over the past three decades that have eroded those labour market institutions that have done much in other countries to mitigate the forces bearing down on pay at the bottom of the labour market... while the particular incidence and composition of low-wage work in any given country is the result of unique patterns of production and employment, we must acknowledge that these patterns are shaped in part by the choices of policymakers.[38]

In other words, the coalition government (and indeed its predecessors to some extent) have deliberately chosen to turn Britain into an increasingly low pay, low skill economy, allowing employers to join a "race to the bottom".

Divide and rule – public vs. private

The pay of people employed in the public sector has been "frozen" as a conscious political plan – to which all the main three political parties have signed up – on the basis that the government can't afford to maintain the real value of the basic pay of key workers like teachers, nurses, firefighters or civil servants. This has meant over a million workers have received a 1% pay "rise", which means (taking inflation into account) a cut in the value of their wages. Once the Office for National Statistics adjusted its figures according to the size of employer, it emerged that public sector workers are now typically paid less than their long-exploited private sector counterparts.[39] The idea that public sector workers are overpaid compared to the private sector has been part of a "divide and rule" strategy, pitting private sector workers against allegedly privileged workers in the public sector to attempt to mask the attack on the incomes and living conditions across the workforce.

Estimates put the loss to the average public sector worker of the four-year imposition of the pay freeze at £3,698, given the rate of inflation – a massive chunk out of the incomes of the "hard-working families" that the political parties claim to represent. Having already kicked away contractual entitlements to pay progression for a number of civil service grades, the coalition delivered a further kick in the teeth for public sector workers by ignoring the recommendations of the NHS pay review, to deny even the meagre 1% rise to people whose contracts entitled them to an incremental progression along the wage scale.[40] George Osborne has spoken of an economy returning to growth, but clearly he hadn't intended public sector workers to enjoy the fruits of recovery.

Performance-related pay – hidden dangers

One favoured mechanism for bringing market incentives into the public sector is to introduce a "performance-related" element into to the way individual workers are paid. Though he was defeated in his attempt to move from national to regional pay bargaining for teachers, Michael Gove nevertheless insisted on introducing a policy which authoritative studies (including by the OECD)[41] have shown has no provable effect in terms of raising standards in education – but does have a provably damaging impact on teachers' morale.

On the face of it, rewarding teachers according to the results they deliver may seem like a good idea. But an educational environment depends on effective teamwork and collaboration between colleagues. A system which incentivises individuals turns a school into a competitive environment, where it is against teachers' interests to share best practice or encourage fellow members of staff. If is only natural that those overlooked for performance-related bonuses are likely to feel resentment at their favoured colleagues. Schools will move further away from mutually supportive, collaborative working environments towards anxious places governed by mutual suspicion.

One of the main problems faced by teachers is that of their excessive workload: the sheer volume of bureaucracy, marking and preparation on top of the hours spent in the classroom. The idea that teachers need to be incentivised to work harder is an insult that flies in the face of the real issues facing the education system. Subjective assessments of performance are also a means by which management can intimidate teachers who might otherwise contemplate taking industrial action to address basic pay levels and structural problems. Since teachers' productivity is hard to measure and compare, the profession will be increasingly geared towards hitting numerical targets such as exam grades, and this can produce perverse incentives to "cherry pick" students and offload difficult cases. Such a target-driven culture distorts educational priorities, turning schools into factories for churning out certain grades but losing the wider role in developing the capacities of all our young people. The introduction of a "payment by results" model in other public services like the NHS, prisons and probation services threatens similarly distorted incentives.

Mind the (pay) gaps

While it is true that on a crude measure (not comparing workers of equivalent levels of skill and experience, or considering the scale of the organisations) the pay of workers in the public sector by 2015 was still slightly ahead of average pay in the private sector, the division is seriously misleading. Workers in the private sector should be aware that attacks on their public sector counterparts are conceived as a general attempt at levelling down pay and conditions across the economy. The public/private distinction had in any case increasingly being eroded by privatisation and outsourcing, which has seen some of the lowest paid workers from the public sector transferred to the private sector, exaggerating wage disparities between the two sectors – but also beginning to level-down standards across the board.

Compared with other significant "pay gaps", the gap between public and private is negligible. By contrast the growing gulf between the incomes of the top 1% and those at the bottom of the earnings distribution has become obscene. So too, more than three decades after the Equal Pay Act, is the gender pay gap. ONS figures showed by 2013 on average men earned 15.7% more than women, up from 14.8% the previous year.[42] There are many factors in operation here, including the distribution of occupations; the existence of a "glass ceiling" where women are not promoted to more senior positions; the greater likelihood of women's career progression being interrupted to have and raise children, and failure to hold adequate equality audits. There also exist significant disparities between earnings across age ranges, as well as between disabled and non-disabled workers, and between white and BAME workers (although the latter category conceals a wide spectrum, with some groups such as Pakistani or African-Caribbean workers disproportionately represented at the bottom end of the income scale).

There is power in a union

The epidemic of low paid jobs[43] has been concentrated especially in sectors like catering in which younger people, women and BAME workers represent a large section of the workforce. The Fast Food Rights/Hungry for Justice campaign launched by BFAWU (part of a global movement against poverty pay, exploitation and the denial of trade union rights in the fast food sector) is a good example of a union actively seeking to organise a highly diverse workforce in an industry notable for its low rates of pay and casualised working conditions.

The only way workers can match the power of the employers is by a system of collective bargaining and that means effective trade unions. The right to collective bargaining has been accepted until fairly recently by most liberal democracies as a legitimate and necessary means of regulating the relationship between employees and those who employ them. Apparently our government no longer believe this. In their paper Reconstruction after the Crisis, John Hendy QC and Keith Ewing, two experts in the law around industrial relations wrote:

> The promotion of collective bargaining is a duty imposed by a series of Treaties ratified by the UK and binding on it. It is a requirement by international law. No government can be permitted to ignore these legal obligations. Britain's failure to protect and extend collective bargaining has made it an international law breaker.

If there remains any doubt on the benefits of strong trade union membership the New Yorker magazine published convincing evidence. Over the latter half of 2014 it covered campaigns waged by their City's fast food workers in their struggle for a living wage. Their reporters discovered that an American fast food worker earns on average $8.9 per hour and half of them are dependent on some form of public assistance. In contrast a Copenhagen Burger King worker makes the equivalent $20 per hour, enjoy five weeks paid holiday a year and a pension. There is no minimum wage in Denmark, instead something much better; strong trade unions. The Burger King employee is protected by an agreement between the 3F union and the employers.[44]

Workers in the UK have been quick to recognise the lessons. The fast food workers' campaign in the UK is demanding not only for a £10/hour National Minimum Wage but, just as importantly, for union recognition at work. The trade union movement needs to take up these multiple inequalities in the fight against exploitation at work. Indeed, evidence suggests that there is a close correlation between the erosion of trade unions and increasing inequality, and that strengthening trade union rights for workers would help to address the emergence of such grotesque inequalities across our society.

Reducing inequality is possible, if you want it

It is a myth that politicians are powerless to limit the rise in inequality. The Equal Pay Act of 1970, the incomes policies pursued in the mid-70s and the introduction of the national minimum wage in 1997 each had an impact in improving the lot of the low paid relative to the rest of society. As predicted in Naomi Klein's essential *The Shock Doctrine*, the big corporate and financial interests which govern society have chosen to use the financial crisis in order to reconfigure the economy to boost their share of the wealth produced by working people.

The project of austerity pursued by the coalition, and shared to a regrettable extent by the Labour "opposition", is designed in part precisely to depress the real share of economic value taken in the form of wages, and to institute a new "flexible" labour market which puts working people at the beck and call of employers.

We have all lost out substantially during the recession – seeing our real wages fall by an average 10% since 2008.[45] We are "recovering" from a significantly weaker position and in conditions where growth in the national economy will not readily translate into recovery in our earnings. Yet the growth of an increasingly casualised labour market characterised by endemic low pay and job insecurity is a product, in part, of political choices. What has been done can be undone. But it will take a determined government prepared to face down the markets and introduce radical policies which end "in-work" poverty and start to make work pay.

The change we need on pay

▶ Increase the National Minimum Wage to £10 per hour, with future increases to be index linked to the prices of a basket of essential goods (see www.realbritainindex.org), and an end to exploitative youth rates

▶ Increase resources for HMRC to pursue more pro-active enforcement measures

▶ Scrap the public sector pay freeze – restore the real value of wages

▶ End the abuse of zero hours contracts

▶ Prevent companies using bogus self-employment and umbrella companies to offload employment costs and deprive workers of key employment rights and protections, or claim tax relief owed to workers

- End workfare schemes – no to coerced unpaid labour
- Ban the advertising of unpaid internships
- Introduce a maximum pay ratio between the highest and lowest paid members of staff, with penalties for aggressive avoidance.

3
Benefits

Most of the Media typically represents benefit claimants as part of an underclass: those too idle to go out to work and content instead to leech off the efforts of hard-working taxpayers. But this picture, which has contributed to a damaging stigma towards benefit claimants, is seriously misrepresentative. The fact that last year over 1,700 people applied for just eight low paid 'barista' roles at Costa Coffee in Nottingham suggests that jobs have not been so easy to find.[1]

In any case, benefits for unemployed people of working age form only a small fraction of the total benefits bill. Out of a total DWP annual budget of £165.6 billion for 2012-13 (the last year for which figures were available), expenditure on Jobseekers' Allowance represented £5.2 billion (3.1%).[2] This was far lower than other items of benefits expenditure, not least the state pension (£79.8 billion, 48.1%)[3] that forms by far the biggest part of welfare spending. As earnings have been squeezed, the welfare system has also started to play an increasingly important role in supporting the incomes of people in work.

Not very generous

By the end of 2014, it was said that in the region of 20 million families "receive some kind of benefit (64 per cent of all families). For 9.6 million families, benefits make up more than half of their entire income."[4] If the taxpayer has been ripped off, it is by

Selected 2012-13 DWP benefit caseloads broken down by family type

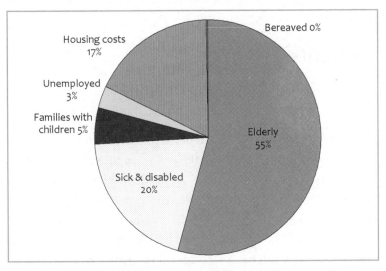

Source: Office for Budget Responsibility: Welfare trends report

employers and landlords whose profits are being subsidised by welfare spending, allowing them to continue to pay poverty wages and hike up rents. In fact, it has been calculated that the failure of employers to pay their workers a living wage is costing the UK Exchequer £6 billion annually,[5] as the welfare system has to step in with working tax credits, child tax credits, housing benefit, and more. At the same time, the system is relatively punitive for those who lose their jobs compared to other EU countries.

The idea that the UK welfare system is so generous that it is inspiring "benefits tourism" is a right-wing myth that has been comprehensively rebutted by economists and social scientists. One way in which this can be measured is the "replacement ratio", which measures how far out-of-work benefits make up for working earnings. Social security expert Declan Gaffney points out[6] that on the OECD's summary table of net replacement ratios, the UK ranked as only 18th out of 24 in the 'generosity' league table. In particularly, Gaffney shows that the UK has been "spectacularly ungenerous compared to other European countries for people who are not long-term unemployed", who form the majority of those experiencing worklessness. Those who lose their jobs and find themselves claiming JSA of £72.40 a week (just £57.35 for those 16-24) are unlikely to feel that the payment is excessively "generous"! According to an opinion poll commissioned by PCS, 79% of people would not be confident of surviving on the current rate of JSA.[7]

Value of benefits declining

In fact, the value of benefits had been declining in relation to average earnings since 1979, when unemployment benefit was around 20% of average earnings. Going into 2015, JSA was worth less than 10%.[8] Plus, as the real value of wages has been squeezed, so too have benefits, which have also risen by less than prices. George Osborne's first move when he became Chancellor was to change the way benefits were indexed to use the lower CPI model of calculating inflation, to take £6 billion from benefit claimants.[9] He followed this by a further £3.7 billion cut over three years by limiting the uprating of most benefits to 1%, effectively committing the government to a year-on-year reduction in the real incomes of some of the poorest in society. This also hits maternity pay and tax credits for the low paid.

Benefits left unclaimed

Given that the cost of essential goods and services had been outstripping general inflation, the effect of this squeeze has hit even harder on those low and modest incomes. The move over recent decades away from universal towards means-tested benefits is estimated to cost eligible claimants some £20 billion,[10] since those most in need of tax credits and means-tested benefit payments are often those least equipped to claim their entitlements.

Benefits cap – social cleansing

Furthermore, the coalition also introduced an overall cap on the total benefits an individual can receive, unless they are in receipt of working tax credits, returning service personnel, on forms of benefit for disabled people accepted as not fit for work or carers entitled to attendance allowance. This has amounted to a maximum of £500 a week for couples or single parents with children living with them, or £350 for single adults without children or whose children live elsewhere. Although this sum (around £26,000 a year) does not seem so bad in most parts of the country, in London and the South East, where average rents are so much higher, many of those hit by the cap are unable to afford to stay in their homes or find alternative affordable accommodation in the city. They have faced being uprooted to places as far away as Hull or Grimsby, miles away from their family and friends – and their children's schools.

The policy's stated intention, to get people off benefits and into employment, has clearly not being fulfilled, since 9 out 10 of those capped had not found a job.[11] Despite the denials of Boris Johnson and Nick Clegg that the result would be widespread "social cleansing", it is clear that the policy was designed to have precisely this effect, by pricing the poor out of the city altogether. In just one of London's 33 boroughs, Brent, the council has relocated 549 households since 2010.[12] There is no reason to believe that it is exceptional in this.

Universal Credit – disaster in waiting

At the time of writing, the project to wrap up six of the major benefits for working age people into Universal Credit – a single payment "masterminded" by Iain Duncan Smith – was seriously behind schedule. Beset by IT failures and administrative complexities, it stands at a risk of becoming an abject and costly failure. In February 2014 it emerged that only 2,720 people had signed up, at a staggering cost of £225,000 per claimant![13] Over a million people were due to be receiving Universal Credit by April, but the numbers had only crept up to just 5,200.

Leaving aside the problems of its implementation, the scheme itself could prove highly problematic for claimants if it is finally delivered. While housing benefit payments could be paid straight to landlords, the Universal Credit will be paid direct to tenants, at a time when they face multiple financial pressures and do not necessarily feel equipped to manage their household budgets. Debt counsellors and social landlords warned that the plan threatens a further sharp increase in levels of rent arrears and evictions, which are already growing because of the hated "Bedroom Tax" – see Chapter 4, Housing.

Punished for working longer

It also appears as though, far from creating incentives for people to get off benefits and find work, Universal Credit would actually penalise people in low paid part-time work (a situation predominantly facing women) who would be worse off if they worked longer hours.

> Take a typical single parent with two children: if she works a day and a half on the minimum wage, it's worth her while and she takes home, with the credit, £268. But if she decides to work three days a week she only earns £6 more. If she goes full-time, she is actually worse off, falling back with £2 less. [Similarly] if one parent is working full-time on the minimum wage taking home £346 a week,

when the other gets a full-time job, their income generally only improves by £29 for her five days at work. (And she earns less full-time than if she worked three days).[14]

As the Joseph Rowntree Foundation has shown, this is a knock-on effect of the limit to benefit upratings, which the government failed to factor into the calculations. It means that tax credits taper off too sharply, leaving perverse incentives in the system. In recognising this, they could have chosen to introduce a more generous tapering effect. However, Duncan Smith is not exactly known for his giving nature and he clearly prefers the stick to the carrot. His preferred option is therefore so-called "in-work conditionality", which in effect means threatening part-time workers who aren't thought to be looking hard enough for more work with the removal of their benefits. This means that the thousands of workers who need extra hours but are unable to find extra shifts will also be punished for living in an economy with high levels of under-employment.

Back to the Poor Law

Whilst focusing on the cost of living lends itself to an emphasis on cuts to benefits, at least as important – if not more so – has been the effect of sanctions, part of a toxic culture which aims to use the threat of withholding benefits to police the behaviour of claimants, leading to cases of destitution for some and inducing fear and anxiety in most.

The original architects of the welfare state saw it as underpinning a universal commitment to basic social security, where people contributed according to their means, risk was shared and every citizen was entitled to help if the circumstances arose. However, neoliberal reform of welfare is designed to end a culture of shared entitlement, in order to create a situation where benefits are privileges the state grants on a conditional basis. Echoing the old Victorian Poor Law, claimants only receive their benefits if they can demonstrate that they are "deserving", while those who are judged undeserving are deprived of even a minimal safety net.

Sanctions – punishing the vulnerable

Under the "reformed" system, Jobseekers can be sanctioned and have their benefits stopped for many reasons. It could be refusing Mandatory Work Activity – that is, if they refuse to be forced into working unpaid doing tasks with no developmental or educational value for a hugely profitable multinational company (see Chapter 2, Pay). Or they can be sanctioned for not attending entirely unproductive interviews with job advisers or training sessions, or for failing to look hard enough for work – even though the jobs don't exist. Or single parents can be sanctioned for looking for part-time rather than full-time work. The 2010 coalition government toughened the sanctions regime, so the minimum period for which benefits are stopped has gone up from one week to four. In the most serious cases benefits can be stopped for up to three years.

In the twelve months to November 2013, the DWP had issued 897,690 sanctions against Jobseekers Allowance and Employment Support Allowance claimants, including over 100,000 against disabled people.[15] The rate of sanctioning also increased, having more than doubled since the coalition came to power in 2010.[16] More than half (58%) of ESA claimants sanctioned are suffering from mental health conditions,[17] indicating that overworked and underpaid Jobcentre Plus (JCP) officials are coming under pressure to apply sanctions (perhaps even to meet specific targets)[18] without the necessary safeguards in place to avoid discrimination. Those being sanctioned in this way have included some very vulnerable people with high support needs, who are understandably confused and alarmed by finding their benefits cut without an explanation. Homeless charity Crisis reports:

> People have told us they have been sanctioned for missing appointments they simply did not know about. This can often be down to late or no notification of appointment dates, with letters going missing in the post or arriving after the scheduled time... Claimants are also being sanctioned or threatened with sanctions for not attending appointments even though they clash with other, sometimes longstanding, commitments. This includes hospital appointments and meetings with probation officers and can happen even when claimants make specific and repeated attempts to notify their advisor of clashes.
>
> It is of particular concern that people are being sanctioned without proper warning or with little or no explanation. Crisis clients on the Work Programme have reported being surprised and shocked that they had been sanctioned after only finding out when they went to sign on at JCP... We are also aware of claimants not being given an explanation as to why they have been sanctioned, even when they make their own enquires. Again, failures in communication between Work Programme providers and JCP are often to blame and sanctioned claimants can become caught between the two, unable to find out why they were sanctioned.[19]

Even where explanations are provided they can be woefully inadequate. Claimants have been sanctioned for missing JCP appointments they only missed in order to attend a job interview![20] Others have been sanctioned for the crime of failing to prove that they looked and applied for enough jobs – on Christmas Day.[21]

The "Stupid Sanctions"[22] Tumblr blog features lots more such "cruel, arbitrary and ridiculous reasons why people have had their benefits stopped".

Thrown into crisis

Statistics show that the incidence of sanctions being appealed is relatively low, but the rate of appeals successfully upheld by an independent tribunal reached an astonishing 9 out of every 10.[23] As Crisis comment:

> Initial decision making is increasingly problematic and decisions are often incorrect. It is therefore essential that everyone who is sanctioned is informed immediately about the new JCP mandatory reconsideration process, and the subsequent route to the appeals and tribunals process. As this does not always happen, it is unlikely that all those sanctioned claimants who should appeal are doing so.

But even where sanctions are successfully appealed, this does not undo the anxiety of being plunged into financial destitution. Where single parents are affected (10% of respondents to a Citizens Advice survey of people who had been sanctioned were lone parents) the potential consequences are particularly devastating, as the household, including dependent children, are forced to subsist on child benefit and child tax credits alone. How do people respond to finding their benefits stopped?

> Respondents coped with the loss of income by borrowing money from friends and family (80%), from the bank or on their credit card (8%) or from a pay day loan company (9%).

They also cut down on food (71%), heating (49%) and travel (47%). Almost a quarter (24%) had applied for a food parcel. Some respondents had been left to scrounge for food from skips or bins, or had had to resort to begging to feed themselves.

The sanction had a severe impact on the mental and physical health of many respondents. Existing health conditions were exacerbated because of poor diet and stress, and a number of respondents said they had attempted suicide or that they felt suicidal.[24]

Benefits sanctioning is also a major driver of the increased need for food banks, with nearly a million visits in 2014, an increase of over 163%. The Trussell Trust, the UK's largest food bank provider, said half of those referred to food banks in 2013-14 were "as a result of benefit delays or changes".[25]

Charities like Crisis are well placed to see how the "catastrophic" (their word) effect of sanctions on claimants can cause homelessness and, ironically, increases the barriers to getting people back into work:

Although not the policy intention, being sanctioned frequently leads to claimants' housing benefit and council tax support claims being stopped. This is a result of claimants not being advised by JCP or their Work Programme provider that they must immediately notify their local authority of a change in circumstances. Without this information, sanctioned claimants face sudden withdrawals of support for housing costs that can lead to arrears, evictions and homelessness...

As well as having an impact on the financial and emotional wellbeing of claimants, sanctions can lead to a breakdown in trust and alienation from JCP, Work Programme providers and services in general putting further barriers in the way of someone finding work. Sanctions therefore undermine the efforts of Crisis and other organisations, who work hard to engage homeless and vulnerable people to help them return to the labour market.

So not only has this aspect of welfare reform a pernicious effect on poor and vulnerable people, it is also incompetent even on its own terms.

The same could also be said for the abolition of the Council Tax Benefit scheme. As a result only pensioners will be automatically protected, with other claimants often becoming liable for between 10-30% of their council tax bill. The new scheme – dubbed "Poll Tax Mark II"[26] makes another 1.9 million claimants – including people on JSA and ESA – liable for paying the tax out of their meagre benefits. This is likely to add further pressure on households struggling to pay the rent, leading to evictions that end up costing councils more in terms of emergency housing payments than they are allegedly "saving" from these changes. For its part, Labour opposed the changes but has not promised to reverse them.

Disabled people – the hardest hit

No group has suffered more heavily from this climate of fear and anxiety in the face of apparently arbitrary judgments than the 11 million disabled people in the UK, together with their families and carers. We know that "disability is one of the key indicators for living in poverty – with estimates of 40% of disabled children living in poverty and a third of disabled adults living in poverty",[27] a situation which will only by made worse by the falling value of benefits. But more than this, the social security and protection that the welfare system used to offer to disabled adults of working age has been thrown into jeopardy with the arrival of the Work Capability Assessment (WCA), where individuals previously entitled to claim Incapacity Benefit now face rigorous tests to see whether they are to qualify for the new Employment and Support Allowance. The so-called "biopsychosocial model" used to justify the scheme has been aggressively promoted by the US private insurance giant Unum, which proposes that

> an emphasis on medical causes and effects has failed to provide an adequate basis for disability benefits policy, and therefore much greater emphasis should be placed on the psychological attitudes and beliefs of individuals. It posits that disability – and the ability to work in particular – is not just a medically definable, physical matter but one that has a social and psychological dimension too. And it is used to underpin the assertion that to a very large extent the growth in the cost of disability benefits must surely be the result of people faking those disabilities. A whole set of workshops run by Unum with such charming titles as 'Malingering and illness deception' should leave us in no doubt about where this approach is coming from.[28]

In the belief that a large number of disabled people are not really incapable of work, it seeks to re-assess them according to what kinds of work they would be able to accomplish rather than what they cannot. Those put in the Work-Related Activity Group of ESA claimants would be subject to the same potential sanctions as JSA claimants if they were not deemed to be making strident enough efforts to find a job. However, this notoriously failed to take into account whether suitable jobs are available, or the chances of employers prioritising disabled applicants, often with complex medical and social needs, over similarly qualified non-disabled candidates. It is also a particularly unsuitable method to judge those who suffer from progressive conditions (whose symptoms may vary from day to day but worsen over time) as well as those suffering from mental health conditions.

The assessments themselves take the form of an IT based tick-box exercise, initially outsourced to French multinational Atos, which soon became hated for its frequently inaccurate and sometimes absurd judgements. The barrage of criticism it attracted would ultimately see the company's contract terminated over a year ahead of its scheduled end after a barrage of criticism that saw even the DWP itself forced to admit "significant quality failures".[29]

Farcically, 31 of Atos's 123 assessment centres lacked ground-floor access for wheelchair users, meaning that thousands of disabled people were physically unable to attend the assessments to which they had been summoned. But where assessments did take place, they frequently came to the wrong conclusions. The experience of GPs, who saw the traumatic effect this experience was having on so many of their patients, saw the British Medical Association call for the WCA to be scrapped.[30] One GP wrote:

> During the past year I have supported appeals for increasing numbers of patients who have had their employment and support allowance (ESA) stopped. Clearly some of the assessments being performed are substandard. All nine of the patients I have supported have successfully appealed against losing the ESA. In every case the assessor failed to appreciate, acknowledge, and record what should have been obvious. None of my patients deserved the extra anxiety and distress that compounded their existing problems.[31]

38% of the decisions were overturned on appeal, but as the Public Accounts Committee has concluded, such "poor decision making causes claimants considerable distress", and the position appears to be getting worse.[32] In taking a case to appeal, claimants are often required to pay for further medical evidence, leading Citizens Advice to point out:

> It is completely unacceptable that sick and disabled people can face charges of more than £100 for medical evidence to help their claim whilst companies delivering assessments can get away without sanction for not doing their job properly.[33]

Worse still, there was no funding available to claimants pending their outcome of their appeals, and no time constraints on the DWP to conduct a further bureaucratic process of "mandatory reconsideration" before the appeal can be heard. Further, the 12-month limit for those on the work-related group of contributory ESA who cannot find work meant that people found themselves without an alternative source of income, disappearing from the radar of the authorities. John McDonnell MP told Parliament that "Some 700,000 disabled people are losing a total of £4.4 billion as a result of the 12-month cut-off."[34]

Tales of woe

John McDonnell was able to secure this debate because campaigners managed to get over 100,000 signatures on the WOW (War on Welfare) petition calling for the abolition of the WCA and an impact assessment looking at the effect of cuts and welfare reforms on sick and disabled people, their families and carers. MPs related some of the horror stories that constituents brought to their weekly surgeries:

Debbie Abrahams (Oldham East and Saddleworth):
I wonder whether my hon. Friend is aware of the case of
one of my constituents. He was receiving ESA, but had a
heart attack during his assessment and was sanctioned as
a result of leaving it.

Jim Sheridan (Paisley and Renfrewshire North):
I was talking with a former Remploy worker who was
about to lose his job. I remember him telling me that he
was fit to work but that his face was so badly disfigured
that he could not go out in public without getting a
terrible reaction. I remember him saying, "Mr Sheridan,
where can I work? Where can I go? If I get on a bus,
people will get off. If I go into a restaurant, people will
walk out. So where do I go?" The only enjoyment that
man had was going out in his disabled person's car to
get some privacy. That was taken away from him. This
is about treating people with respect and dignity. The
people who conduct the Atos assessments do not take
those things into consideration.

Simon Danczuk (Rochdale):
I want to read out a letter that was recently received by
one of my constituents:
"Dear Miss Holt,
You are now approaching the end of the 1st Stage of
your Intensive Job Focused Activity. We hope that all the
activity or training intervention completed so far has not
only supported you to achieve your aspirations but has
moved you closer to the job market.
You will shortly enter the 2nd Stage of your Intensive Job
Focused activity.
Sessions and Workshops may vary depending on the
centre you attend."

The letter was sent to my constituent Sheila Holt on 30 January. I am sad to have to inform the House that Sheila will not be able to attend the second stage of her intensive job-focused activity because she has been in a coma since December. Members of her family have repeatedly informed the DWP and Seetec that she is not well, but those organisations have continued to harass them.[35]

Newspapers were littered with absurd and tragic examples of terminally-ill people being found "fit for work". As Ian Mearns told his fellow MPs:

Between January 2011 and November 2011, some 10,600 employment and support allowance claims ended and a date of death was recorded within six weeks of the claim end. This government have repeatedly refused to release updated 2013 statistics on deaths within six weeks of the end of an ESA claim, calling such requests for information "vexatious". Four people a day are dying within six weeks of being declared fit for work under the WCA – it is scandalous and an indictment of this place.[36]

It is scarcely any surprise that 84% of GPs have reported patients with "mental health problems, such as stress, anxiety and depression as a result of undergoing or the fear of undergoing the work capability assessment".[37]

In addition to the trauma of the WCA, disabled people have also been disproportionately hit by other benefit cuts. As McDonnell continued:

Disabled people... will be disproportionately hit by the bedroom tax. Some 72% of affected households include someone with a disability or major health problem, and

420,000 disabled people will lose on average £14 a week in housing benefit. One in three disabled people is refused the discretionary housing payment. Shockingly, local councils have rejected applications from disabled people living in adapted properties who are unable to downsize. Last week, it was also revealed that the £347 million local welfare assistance fund to local councils had quietly been cut by the government.

The Welfare Reform Act 2012 also changed the uprating of benefits basis from the retail prices index to the consumer prices index, costing some families receiving DLA and the carer's allowance £80 a week. It has been estimated that 142,500 disabled people will be hit by the benefit cap, costing £2 billion...

What do all these figures add up to? Although the government have refused to undertake a cumulative assessment of the effect of all the benefit changes on disabled people, others have done so. The Demos-Scope study ["Coping with the Cuts"] calculated that disabled people will lose £28.3 billion by 2018. Dr Simon Bamber concludes that disabled people in poverty, who make up 4% of the population, will bear 13% of the cuts and lose £4,660 a year. People using social care who make up 3% of the population will also bear 13% of the cuts, and lose £6,409 a year.

It doesn't even end there. The Disability Living Allowance and Independent Living Fund – not work-related benefits but payments to support sick and disabled people with their support needs and higher than average living costs, crucial if they are able to live in their own homes – were being replaced by a new benefit, the Personal Independence Payment. Analysts estimated that 600,000 people would be impacted by the introduction of PIP, with a total loss of £2.6 billion.[38] This includes 148,000 who would lose out from changes to the eligibility criteria for the mobility component of DLA. This might mean, for example, that they would no longer have access to a Motability vehicle – meaning, ironically, that amongst other things they will be unable to get to work.

PIP – beset with difficulties

As with Universal Credit, the roll-out of PIP had been beleaguered with difficulties. A National Audit Office report stated:

> Backlogs have developed at each stage of the claimant process... The Department had made only 16% of the number of decisions it expected, over 166,000 people had started new claims for Personal Independence Payment and 92,000 claims had been transferred to the assessment provider and not yet returned to the Department.[39]

Perhaps we should not to be too surprised by the extent of the delays given that the assessment providers were Capita, together with – unbelievably, given their role in the WCA fiasco – Atos. Caroline Lucas told her fellow MPs of the impact this was having on her constituents in Brighton and Hove:

> [The cancer charity] Macmillan relayed the story of Mr J, a 32-year-old who is suffering from advanced bowel cancer and who came to the charity for help. It took more than 10 weeks for him to be assessed. His wife was acting as his full-time career because he was so ill. She was also looking after their baby and young child. The report states: "Throughout this process both Mr and Mrs J were very anxious and suffering serious

financial hardship. Mr J at this time was seriously ill, vomiting day and night plus major issues re fatigue due to chemotherapy etc. Both also felt throughout the period that they were not believed and had been labelled scroungers and benefit cheats by the DWP."

The work by Advice Brighton and Hove makes it clear that people who are applying for PIP – some of the most vulnerable people – are being left without adequate finances. That is having a massive impact on their physical and emotional well-being.

It is clear from the above examples that "welfare reform" has been having a devastating impact on the living standards of disabled people, not only in financial terms but also in terms of quality of life. Sick and disabled people have not only been treated abysmally by reforms to the welfare system, but have also been disproportionately affected by austerity cuts to spending.

The ultimate price

People have been finding themselves in greater need of adult social care support at precisely the time when it is being slashed by local authorities facing vast cuts to their budgets.

By next month, £2.68 billion will have been cut out of adult social care budgets across the country. In 2012-13, 320,000 fewer disabled people and 37,000 fewer adults aged between 18 and 64 with physical impairments received local authority care and support than in 2005-06... A recent inquiry by the all-party groups on local government and on disability found from the evidence they took that four in 10 disabled people are failing to have their basic social care needs met.[40]

Tragically, the extreme levels of turmoil caused to vulnerable people by the prospect of being thrown into abject poverty and destitution has also claimed the lives of people who, seeing no future for themselves or those around them, have resorted to suicide. Calum's List details 30 fatalities where welfare reforms have been at least in part to blame.[41] This is what happens when people are driven to feel that living comes at too high a price.

Were there any signs of hope on the horizon? There has been little evidence that the coalition parties either know or care about the devastating effects their policies are having. Their morally bankrupt reforms have drawn wide criticism even from senior faith leaders, appalled at these callous attacks on the poor and vulnerable. But what can we expect from a Labour government? Sadly, before the 2015 general election the Labour Party were equally desperate to show how "tough" they will be on welfare. The announcement that benefits will be taken away from young jobseekers if they fail to engage in training schemes (however unsatisfactory or inappropriate they might be to the needs of that young person) was another example of a policy designed to cut costs by punishing the poor, rather than genuinely helping people into worthwhile employment. In vote after vote in Parliament – from refusing to vote against the legal changes the Tories need to keep going with workfare to supporting the idea of an overall cap on benefits spending – Labour showed that it remains on board with the overall philosophy of the attack on the welfare state, even if it criticises some aspects of its implementation by the coalition.

A Citizens Income – towards a radical alternative

The benefits system in the UK is broken, and the public discourse around welfare has become utterly toxic. Stigmatising attitudes and punitive treatment are now hardwired into the programme of "reform", which is returning us to the pernicious discourse of the deserving and undeserving poor. The draconian culture of sanctions means that it is possible to be a citizen of one of the world's wealthiest economies in the 21st century and yet still face total destitution, forced to depend on charity for the most basic sustenance. The system of means-testing is complex and bureaucratic, leads to people failing to claim benefits to which they are properly entitled, and is poorly equipped to deal with fluctuating circumstances. Meanwhile, perverse incentives still abound, and the new "Universal Credit" intended to iron out some of these complexities is increasingly regarded as unworkable.

The idea of a Citizens Income (also known as an Unconditional Basic Income, or Basic Income) would offer the chance to reconfigure a social security based on universal entitlement. Essentially, it would guarantee each individual citizen – as of right – a basic flat-rate level of income on which it is possible to get by. The whole panoply of means-testing, allowances, tax credits, sanctions and "benefit traps" would be a thing of the past, as people would automatically qualify for a basic minimum level of economic security irrespective of their changing circumstances. Clearly there are questions about implementation and affordability which require detailed investigation. But the general principle of moving away from a system which requires people to demonstrate that they are sufficiently deserving of a basic income is surely a more civilised and socially just form of collective social provision.

The change we need on benefits

▸ Uprate all benefits at least in line with inflation
▸ Abolish arbitrary caps on the overall benefit spend – benefits should be paid according to need

▶ Stop privatisation and outsourcing of the administration of welfare, and bring assessments and support services back in-house

▶ End the culture of sanctions – introduce positive incentives for claimants

▶ Scrap the Work Capability Assessment, and remodel support for sick and disabled people taking into account the barriers to, and support necessary for, finding and sustaining employment

▶ Bring down the bill for in-work benefits by increasing the national minimum wage to at least £10 per hour (or the Living Wage, whichever is the greater), so public funds no longer subsidise employers paying poverty wages, and scrap exploitative youth rates

▶ Bring down the housing benefit bill by capping private rents, ending the subsidy to landlords, and protecting people from the individual benefit cap

▶ Invest in a green jobs creation programme to bring down the levels of people claiming unemployment benefits

▶ Properly reward family and community care work

▶ Prepare a wide-ranging feasibility study to assess how we could implement a basic minimum Citizen's Income.

4

Housing

Britain is in the grip of a housing crisis, and it is going to get worse. A tiny handful of overseas investors, property speculators and banking bosses have pocketed millions from the profits that can be made where supply remains suppressed whilst demand and prices continue to soar. 107,950 homes were built in the year to April 2013, less than half the 250,000 to 300,000 that housing experts claim are needed just to stand still.[1]

The number of "affordable" homes; defined as properties at 80% or less of market rate – in reality well beyond what many families can afford – fell by as much as 26% to an eight-year low.[2] New home building by local authorities has virtually stopped altogether.

House price bubble

Meanwhile, we have been exposed to billions in liabilities for the government's Help to Buy scheme, which is bringing back the possibility of taking out mortgages on the massive loan-to-value (LTV) ratios that wreaked so much havoc in the financial crisis. The temporary gains for a few first-time buyers and property developers has come at the expense of a growing housing bubble, with rocketing prices taking home ownership beyond the reach of hundreds of thousands each year. Analysts forecast that house prices could shoot up by 35% by 2020, with rents forecast to soar by 39% over the same period.[3] Much of the development that does take place is of luxury flats, bought off-plan by overseas investors.

The resulting situation has been one of misery for most households in Britain. Housing charity Shelter reported in 2014 that:

▸ 1.4 million people in Britain are falling behind with their rent or mortgage payments.

▸ The number of people struggling to pay their rent or mortgage each month has increased by 44% over the past year, to 7.8 million people.

▸ Almost a million people used a payday loan to help pay their rent or mortgage.

▸ 2.8 million people used an unauthorised overdraft to help pay their rent or mortgage, and of those 10% did so every month.[4]

▸ Almost one in three adults (around 15 million people) say housing costs are causing stress and depression in their family.

▸ One in four (around 12 million people) are kept awake at night by the stress of paying their rent or mortgage.

▸ One in four say housing costs are causing arguments with their partner and other family members.[5]

Those fortunate enough to own their own homes outright have found that their children cannot afford to buy a home of their own, while those with mortgages are already having difficulty making the repayments and face the possibility of financial wipe-out in the event of interest rate hikes. Social renters have faced increasing risks of evictions with government benefit changes and rising rents, while others – marooned on long social housing waiting lists and unable to save enough for a deposit – are forced to live with their parents into their 30s, or else move into the private rented sector and either take low-quality housing or see a huge percentage of their income go on housing costs, making saving all but impossible.

Running down council housing

In the belief that rising prices are both electorally popular and the main way of persuading private interests to build, governments since 1979 have failed to address the structural crisis in housing supply, and actively encouraged market-based solutions based on competition. The Thatcher government in particular sought to foster greater levels of owner-occupation and private rentals at the expense of maintaining and expanding council housing, and depleted social housing stock through the "right to buy". The outcome of the sale of council houses was not only the obvious one, a disastrous drop in the supply of social housing. The cost of this fire-sale of public assets has too often been overlooked. In many cases council houses were not sold, they were practically given away. Thatcher's 'generosity' in giving away what was not hers to give, was socially divisive. Those who had longstanding council tenancies could snap up a cheap deal, but those who had lived in privately-rented accommodation for the same period were offered no such help onto the housing ladder.

We are all still paying for this. Many of those properties are once again available for rent, but from private landlords at the 'commercial rate'. Two neighbours, living in exactly the same kind of property, one tenant of the council or housing association, the other renting from a private landlord will soon discover a difference. They are paying very different rents. This is not only unjust, the contrasts have another significance, If the private tenant falls on hard times and has to claim housing benefit, the cost in public funds far exceeds the amount due to a council tenant.

The Tories also scrapped rent controls and introduced new Assured Shorthold Tenancies, a deregulation of the private rental market which – together with rising property prices – further encouraged landlords and banks to invest in rental property as a form of speculation. New Labour's introduction of tax reliefs on people buying second homes to let helped allow widespread small-scale speculation in private rental properties. The result was an acceleration of house prices and a growing number of people who, unable to find a home of their own, are forced to rent from a private landlord.

Generation Rent

The losers are those who make up "Generation Rent". As *PricedOut*, the campaign group for those unable to get onto the property ladder, argues:

> Housing across much of the UK has become unaffordable for ordinary people, as successive governments encourage people to treat houses as investments rather than somewhere to live. As a result of rising house prices it now takes 12 years on average to save a deposit.[6]

Median house prices rose by 249% from 1997 to 2012, in comparison with a growth in earnings of just 51%.[7] While the problem has been particularly acute in London and the South East, every region of the UK saw house prices outstrip inflation and wages during this period. The real cost of housing did fall somewhat in the wake of the financial crisis, but housing did not become more affordable since, as we have seen, real incomes were also badly hit during this period. Annual house price inflation is running at 9% (up to 17.7% in London). To put this staggering rate of inflation in context, housing charity Shelter has calculated that, had the price of everyday groceries risen as rapidly as house prices from 1971-2011, we would now be paying £51.18 for a chicken, and £10.45 for a 4-pint carton of milk![8]

Unaffordable

Many young people are relying on financial assistance from the "bank of Mum and Dad", with parents forking out £2 billion a year to help out their children get onto the housing ladder.[9] But for those whose parents do not have deep pockets the outlook is bleak. The latest English Housing Survey shows that overall levels of homeownership fell to their lowest level since 1987, now standing at 65.2%, down from 71% in 2003.[10]

The contraction in bank lending and curb on high LTV mortgage lending following the banking crisis, prevented first-time buyers taking out a mortgage. Those who stretched themselves to afford their mortgage are finding themselves potentially over-exposed to the risk of higher interest rates, with 14% of mortgage-payers telling a survey by the Building Societies Association that a 1% increase in the Bank of England base rate would give them difficulty making their repayments.[11] "One in six households has become mortgaged to the hilt, servicing home loans that are at least four times the size of their annual salary" reports the *Guardian*.[12]

Mortgaged to the hilt

Further, the Resolution Foundation, using official statistics from the Office of Budget Responsibility (OBR), has calculated that an increase of 5% in interest rates by 2018 could lead to around two million households being plunged into financial trouble and at risk of having their properties repossessed, with half of these being families with children.[13]

As they commented:

> Even if we take a somewhat rosy view of how the economy will develop over the next few years, the number of households severely exposed to debt looks as though it will double... the levels of debt built up by families in the pre-crisis years are such that even relatively modest changes in incomes and borrowing cost assumptions produce significantly worse outcomes.[14]

So to think that many of those fortunate enough to have become homeowners are on a one-way gravy train to prosperity is hugely misleading and overlooks the inherent risk that high LTV mortgage lending has delivered. The Help to Buy scheme may have transferred risk from the lending institution to public funds and held out the prospect of "easy access" credit to first-time buyers, but it has done nothing to address the underlying structural reasons for the increasing unaffordability of home ownership. In fact it was only accelerating the affordability gap that is either stretching families to the limit or else making people abandon the prospect of homeownership altogether. One recent survey of 2,000 under-35s found that, despite Help to Buy, "around 70 per cent of those saving for a deposit have become so disillusioned that they have abandoned the effort and spent the money on holidays, cars, or simply to cover the bills... half have 'given up all hope' of every owning a property."[15]

That many young people are reaching this conclusion is not surprising. Although the Help to Buy scheme is offering some temporary assistance to first-time buyers, most lenders are still demanding a higher deposit relative to the property's value than before the crisis. 63% of would-be first time buyers cite finding the cash for the deposit as the biggest barrier to owning their own home.[16] Modelling for Shelter, factoring in the relative changes to inflation, earnings and house prices, calculates that even a two-earner couple without children would take 11 years to save enough for a deposit in London, and nearly a decade to take out a mortgage in Brighton and Hove, Bath and North East Somerset, Devon, Cornwall, Surrey or Hereford. Further:

> ... across much of England couples with a child may not have saved a sufficient deposit to buy a home until their child is into their early or mid-teens. For couples with more than one child, homeownership is likely to be even less achievable. For single person households, the picture is even starker. It is estimated to take a single person more than a decade to save for a deposit in 114 of the 150 counties and unitary authorities in England (76%). It could take longer than 15 years in 53 (or 35%) of these local areas.[17]

If prices continue on the current trajectory, the report added, "soon more than half of typical double-earning families will not have managed to get on the ladder by the age of 65, and fewer than 1 in 5 would be able to become owners in London".[18] By 2015, the average home in the UK costs 5.5 times the average income, rising to a record 8 times higher in London.

PricedOut has calculated that since George Osborne announced Help to Buy, stimulating an 8% increase in house prices, 245,000 had been priced out of being able to afford a home, compared to the 20,000 who have been able to take advantage of the scheme, with a further 160,000 priced out by the end of 2014.[19]

Stable prices needed

The assumption that rising housing prices are both politically popular and economically positive is highly questionable. 66% of respondents to a recent YouGov survey wanted house prices to fall or stay the same, with only 25% wanting them to rise – a pattern which was replicated in all parts of the country. Even those who own their own home outright responded similarly.[20] Of course people are happy to see their own home go up in value relative to the rest of the market. Yet at the same time they recognise that general rises in prices are not desirable, if for example it means that future generations are locked out of home ownership altogether. Nor is there some intrinsic economic advantage to rising house prices. Countries that have seen relatively stable housing prices, such as Germany, have economies better able to withstand the financial crisis than those that were more exposed to the aggressive expansion of housing credit. As Shelter point out:

> During the 1950s and 1960s, before the era of rapid house price inflation even began, we were able to build up to four times as many new homes per year as we have done in recent years. Equally, in the years of most rapid house price inflation (1997-2003) we were building record low numbers of homes.[21]

Letting the market rip is what has given us this housing crisis; more of the same is a recipe for disaster.

What is an "affordable" rent?

A major driver of the current housing crisis has been the failure to build enough homes over recent decades to keep pace with growing demand. Local authorities have not been given the power to invest in new council homes, and the private sector has not built at sufficient levels – in part because of "land-banking", where investments in land can be relied upon to appreciate in value without the risk of actually building any homes.

The government's "solution" to the problem of building more affordable homes has been to cut levels of direct investment, allowing housing associations and private developers to capitalise new developments for the social rented sector, and allowing them to market the properties at an intermediate level of "affordable" rents (up to 80% of the going market rate). The projects' higher rents would help to finance the developments, lowering the need for up-front public spending. This means that housing associations will be stretched in terms of the amount they are forced to borrow, and hence vulnerable either to any further shock in the housing market or changes to their rental income as tenants affected by welfare reforms fall into arrears.

The end of council housing?

The new model of "flexible" social rents encourages fixed-term rather than permanent letting. While the new rents and tenure limits won't apply to existing social tenants directly, only to new lets in the first instance, there will be pressure over time to re-let only at "affordable" rates rather than current social rents. There has already been pressure on hard-pressed local authorities to pursue a policy of rent convergence up towards a new level of "target rent". These policies have already been forcing up a housing benefit budget which threatens to spiral out of control, and the overall benefits cap will mean that for many Londoners the so-called "affordable" homes are anything but.

What stands to be undermined (perhaps fatally) is the existence of social housing as offering a kind of security of tenure otherwise inaccessible to those priced out of owner-occupation. The Tories have made little secret about their intention to move away from a model where social housing offers lifetime tenure to tenants in favour of a model where limited-term tenures offer only a temporary safety net. Rather than address the long-term crisis in undersupply of social housing by allowing local authorities to build new council homes, the coalition sought to undermine the rights of existing tenants in order to socially engineer the usage of the current inadequate stock to limit what they view as "under-occupancy".

Bedroom Tax – an attack on security of tenure

The result was the hated Bedroom Tax, where social tenants face reductions in their housing benefit for having rooms that are deemed to be "spare" – 14% for one "spare" room, 25% for two or more. In reality the extra rooms are often vital to maintain tenants' quality of life – for single parents without custody to allow their children to visit occasionally, to allow disabled people to store wheelchairs or other medical equipment, or to allow the sick room to recuperate. Some of the rooms deemed "spare" may have been specially adapted for the needs of the tenants, for example to provide a dedicated "sensory space" for an autistic child to rest. Under the strict criteria, children of the same sex under 16 are not allowed their own bedrooms and children of different sexes have to share rooms until they are at least 10 years old.

No smaller homes to move into

What makes the policy all the more vicious is that there simply is not enough one or two-bedroom properties available for people to downsize into. In Newcastle, for example, there were said to be 7,000 people "over-occupying" two-bedroom flats, yet just 50 one-bed flats were available. What were the other 6,950 meant to do? Stay in their homes but fall behind on the rent, or perhaps skip meals or turn off the heating? Turn to payday lenders? Or move into the private sector,

The personal cost

What advocates of the Bedroom Tax either don't see or don't care about is that these are not just interchangeable spaces to be swapped in and out of at will. They are homes, in which people have built up emotional investments. Take Bridget, a woman a few years before pensionable age whose children had grown up in the house before moving away, and whose husband had recently died of cancer, his ashes buried in the back garden he used to love. Technically she now had 2 "spare" rooms and so suddenly faced a 25% reduction in her housing benefit, – money which on a low income she simply could not find. Even if an available one-bedroom property could be found, is it really a matter of no real importance to ask her to leave her home of three decades or more?

Or take Herbert, a single West Indian man in his forties with mental health needs, who some years ago agreed to move into a three-bed property near the top of a high-rise council block – hardly suitable for a mum struggling with kids or a pram – since no one-beds where available in the local area. Having come to regard the property as home, he now faces a similar dramatic cut to his already meagre income.

where higher rents would push up the cost to the taxpayer and eliminate the promised "savings" to the housing benefit bill? We know from a National Housing Federation survey that two-thirds of households affected by the bedroom tax have fallen into rent arrears, with one in seven having received notices of eviction.[22] This is even factoring in the use of discretionary housing payments (DHP); a temporary source of funding that has allowed councils to cushion the burden as far as possible.

When this help dries up, the situation is set to become much worse still. The resulting shortfall in rental income has been having an impact on the budgets of both local authorities and registered social landlords, which is likely to mean that even those tenants exempt from paying the Bedroom Tax directly will nevertheless feel the impact in terms of the reduction in maintenance and repairs to their properties. Meanwhile, in the absence of significantly more genuinely affordable properties, the waiting lists for social housing have been continuing to grow.

Expansion of private renting

The net result of the crisis we have described in both the affordability of home ownership and the scarcity of available properties at social rents has been a massive increase in the numbers of people forced into the private rented sector. We witnessed a colossal increase in the private rented sector of 134% in the period 1991-2011, and more than 10 million people (4 million households) are now in privately rented accommodation, 17% of all UK households.[23] In the last decade alone the numbers renting from a private landlord has leapt by 69%.[24] This closely tracks the massive increase in house prices over the same period.

Although the private rental market is useful to some people who want the convenience of short-term tenancies and the flexibility to move around, a growing majority of private renters are stuck with no other option since they can neither afford a mortgage nor access social housing. Accordingly, the make-up of those renting privately is changing. Today, "a third of renting households are families with children, and half of households renting are 35 or older".[25] So what are the disadvantages faced by this new "Generation Rent"?

Soaring cost of renting

Firstly, renting from a private landlord is very costly, and increasingly more so. Rents have been on the increase in 83% of local authority areas, and in every area of the country other than the North East.[26] Shelter's report *The Rent Trap* explains:

> The average rent on a home is more costly than paying a mortgage in every region of England, even after accounting for homeowners' repair and maintenance costs. Government statistics show that renters pay an average of £75 more a month than people with a mortgage, yet renters typically earn less than home owners.[27]

Nearly half (49%) of respondents to a YouGov survey said they received "poor or very poor value for money" from renting privately.[28] High rents have been seriously eating into incomes, with the typical family in London having to fork out an average 59% of their income in rent.[29] Clearly, costs on this scale make saving towards a deposit on a home difficult or impossible. As Shelter reported:

> Renting families on average have £179 a month after paying rent and other essentials. But more than half of renting families have £50 or less left over... 81% of renting families say they are able to save £50 or less each month from the money left over after essentials, and the average is just £63 a month ... 58% are unable to set aside any money for saving each month.[30]

Given that the average deposit on a house had already reached £26,500 (in London, a shocking £72,760)[31] by 2013 it is clear how far most families in private rented accommodation are from home ownership. The impact this has been having on the lives of millions cannot be underestimated.

Rip-off agencies

But the rip off does not end there; private tenants have to run the gamut of the poorly-regulated residential lettings agency market. Over 60% of tenancies in England involve a letting agency, contracted by the landlord to find a suitable tenant and often to manage the property. If prospective tenants want a particular property, they have little choice but to deal with the letting agency marketing it and little power to negotiate over terms. In addition to asking for a deposit and at least a month's rent in advance, letting agencies will often charge additional and unpredictable hidden fees:

> Tenants renting from a letting agency are most likely to be charged an admin fee (70%), initial contract fee (62%), or credit check (52%) ... There are widespread concerns that fees are not made clear enough to tenants early enough in the lettings process. Fewer than half (43%) of all renters surveyed for Shelter said that their letting agency was open and transparent about the fees they would be asked to pay.[32]

All this would be bad enough if tenants only felt fleeced by letting agents on a one-off basis. But since most shorthold tenancies are only for periods of 6 or 12 months, there is every chance of repeat fees.

This whole experience points to a further major downside of private renting, namely the uncertainty of tenure, with tenants haunted by the possibility of being given just a couple of months to quit or finding themselves subject to an unaffordable hike in their rents. The experience of flat-hunting is stressful enough even for the young and unattached, but for families with young children the prospect of having to undergo several disruptive moves in relatively short succession is frightening.

Poor conditions and "beds in sheds"

Another key drawback to private renting is that the most affordable properties are also the most likely to be poor living environments. The most recent English Housing Survey showed that a third of homes (1.3 million) in the private rented sector failed to meet the government's Decent Homes Standard (more than double the rate of the social rented sector), with 18.9% being reported as constituting a Category 1 (serious) hazard.[33] Shelter's research shows that:

> 61 per cent of tenants have experienced at least one of the following problems in the last 12 months: mould or damp; leaking roofs or windows; electrical hazards; animal infestations or a gas leak.[34]

The landlords in question might be outright rogue operators, determined to extract the maximum possible rent at the lowest possible cost to themselves with no thought whatever to the safety and health of their tenants. Or they might just be ignorant or ill-equipped landlords unaware of their responsibilities, the extent of the problem or the action needed to put it right. But the tenant has little power in relation to a landlord who refuses to make the necessary repairs.

Local authorities do have the power to compel landlords to act. But they generally rely on responding to complaints, and currently only around 8% of renters have made official complaints.[35] The problem of under-reporting is no doubt partly because they fear that landlords will evict them for insisting on improvements, given the relative lack of protections in law.

The lack of access to decent housing can be compounded by the increasing overcrowding of privately let properties due to the crisis of affordability. This is a particular problem for migrant workers exploited by rogue landlords, for example trying to bypass planning laws by charging people for sleeping in overcrowded temporary structures, known as "beds in sheds". Some councils like the London Borough of Newham have looked to introduce a licensing scheme for private landlords, although there are concerns about the way this has been linked to the policing of the immigration system.

No home of their own

But even where there is accommodation, the prospect of having to share a home out of financial necessity rather than choice has been another growing problem for "Generation Rent". This is particularly the case since the government increased the threshold for which single adults could qualify for housing benefit on a flat of their own to 35.

Research for homelessness charity Crisis shows that "fewer than 2% of properties are now available and affordable for single young people on housing benefit in the private rented sector, despite ministers saying that the cheapest third of properties should be".[36] Thus for many the student-style flat-share is not something they can leave behind on graduation, but a matter of necessity which they face into their mid-30s. As we have seen few of those renting privately can afford to buy a home of their own, so even this option is bought at the price of delaying – perhaps permanently – the prospect of home ownership. No doubt this helps to explain why around 3.3 million (1 in 4) young adults between 20-34 now live with their parents.[37]

This situation has been cited by young people as a cause of stress on the family and leading to relationship difficulties. This problem could be made worse still if the mooted Tory plan to abolish housing benefit entitlement for under-25s comes in. As Crisis explains:

> About 380,000 people aged under 25 are currently supported by housing benefit. Of these, 204,000 are parents (mostly single mothers), at least 66,000 are working, and 28,000 are sick or disabled and claiming ESA. Around a quarter (99,000) are looking for work. There are many reasons some young people cannot live at home. Their parents may have died. There may not be enough space, or indeed they might have moved away to look for or take up work. They may have suffered abuse at home, or have simply been told they are not welcome to stay or move back in. Latest government statistics show that 10,000 people were accepted as homeless last year because their parents would not or could not house them.[38]

Those unable to find even a shared affordable property are becoming part of an epidemic of young homeless people.

Housing benefit – gravy train for landlords

The housing benefit bill stood at £23 billion last year, and is projected to rise still further given the expansion of the private rented sector. But if the government wants to cut the overall bill then their approach is exactly the *wrong* way to go about it, since it punishes the poor and vulnerable for their poverty whilst doing nothing to address the underlying structural causes of the rocketing costs. In effect the present system provides a lavish subsidy to private landlords, "buy-to-let" speculators and property tycoons amounting to £9.2 billion per year,[39] allowing them to hike rents beyond what millions can afford.

Indeed, as research by the *Daily Mirror* and GMB union based on Freedom of Information requests to local authorities shows, housing benefit payments hand millions directly to landlords. It reported that the Britain's richest MP, the Tory Richard Benyon (a critic of the welfare system) was making £625,000 from housing benefit each year. Similarly, Lord Cavendish benefitted from £106,938 in housing welfare last year from Barrow council in Cumbria through his shareholding in Holker Estates and the Earl Cadogan, who has given £23,000 to the Tories, has received £116,400 in benefits from Kensington and Chelsea.[40] These are the real "benefit scroungers" ripping off the hardworking taxpayer. If we are going to tackle the housing crisis we need bold policy solutions which can tackle the crisis in supply and start to get genuinely affordable houses built in the right places, hold down rents, bring down the welfare bill by making sure it benefits tenants rather than landlords, begins to stabilise house prices and deflate the housing bubble.

Labour has so far taken only small, hesitating steps in this direction. Labour has committed to building 200,000 more homes a year, which is welcome, although it is not clear what percentage will be genuinely affordable and there is no commitment to an expansion in council house-building. Plans to extend security of tenure and ban excessive lettings charges are welcome but limited. Most tellingly, while the announcement of a cap on mid-tenancy rent rises by landlords is positive, this is simply a policy to limit the further growth in already intolerable levels of unaffordability, since rents are already astronomically high compared to incomes. What it will not deliver is the comprehensive package of rent controls that we would need to end the lavish subsidy to landlords via housing benefit and fully reset the rental market to the advantage of the renter.

The change we need on housing

▶ Allow local authorities to build council houses and borrow more to invest in this vital infrastructure and commit to a national house-building programme of publicly owned stock to guarantee that at least 300,000 genuinely affordable properties are built each year, with the emphasis on environmentally sustainable planning and building

▶ Scrap Help to Buy but use the public stake in high street banks to provide low-cost lending, including mortgages, and allow councils to borrow to take out an equity stake in first home purchases, to be repaid via rent repayments

▶ Scrap the Bedroom Tax and retain housing benefit for under 25s

▶ Reinstate the Council Tax Benefit scheme abolished by the coalition

▶ Reintroduce effective rent controls

▶ Houses are for living in, not speculation – introduce punitive taxes on second homes and all further homes

▶ Abolish the "right to buy" council housing

▶ Introduce a land value tax on the unearned income accruing to landowners and developers

▶ Stop land-banking by allowing the compulsory purchase of land where development has yet to begin within 12 months of planning permission being granted, or after 12 months has expired with no planning permission being sought

▶ Introduce an effective licensing scheme for private landlords to drive up standards, acting wholly independently from policing of the immigration system

▶ Establish a national publicly-owned letting agency operating on a not-for-profit basis

▶ All new housing developments to contain a minimum number for rent at no higher than the rate of social rents and contain shared public space and community facilities.

5

The Cost of Borrowing

The economic growth of the 1990s and 2000s lacked firm foundations. It was built on the expansion of financial services that were too dependent on unsustainable levels of consumer credit. Notoriously, the US "sub-prime debt" market involved banks massively expanding irresponsible mortgage lending to people who would never be in a position to repay, while concealing this basic economic fact with ever more complex and opaque forms of financial engineering. The years of growth had been paid for on the never-never, and sure enough the day of reckoning came with a vengeance when the global financial crisis hit in 2008.

Maxed out

On the eve of the crash, in the first quarter of 2008, Britain's national household debt ratio stood at 170%, a historic high.[1] Spending-led economic growth was built on consumer spending, with people "maxing out" their credit cards and banks prepared to lend on mortgages with worryingly high loan-to-value ratios. As the deep recession hit, the household debt ratio started to fall, with worried families trying to limit their exposure to debt by going without holidays or home improvements and prioritising just paying the bills. Before the recovery began, the household debt ratio was 138%.[2]

Debt-fuelled growth

However, the return to (very modest) growth has been built on a return to business-as-usual, with the debt ratio set to have hit 160% of income by 2018,[3] partly as a result of policies like Help to Buy producing a housing bubble and underwriting additional mortgage debt. However, in absolute terms household debt has already surpassed its 2008 peak, with the total value of UK consumers' debts amounting to a colossal £1,429,624,000,000 (nearly £1.43 trillion), an average of £28,489 for every adult in the UK.[4] The Resolution Foundation claims that the present nascent recovery is flying on the single engine of household spending power; business investment has remained stagnant – very different to the scenario that followed the 1980s and 1990s recessions".[5]

Household spending and business investment after recessions

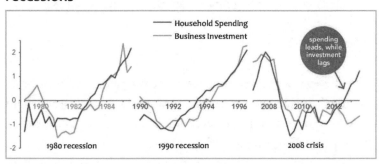

Source: Resolution Foundation

For a recovery to be sustainable, it cannot be driven by spending alone. Not only has business investment remained largely stagnant, but people have also been forced to eat into their savings – where they exist. Since the second quarter of 2009, the UK savings ratio has now fallen from 8.6 per cent to 5.4 per cent ... A falling savings ratio cannot continue indefinitely. Either business investment rebounds, household incomes quickly recover, or else the depletion of savings – and with it the recovery – will run out of road.[6]

At the same time, the impact of the crisis on the distribution of wealth has been markedly unequal:

> Among mortgagors, net worth – savings, shares and property wealth – fell across the bottom 80 per cent of people from 2005 to 2013 but rose for the top 20 per cent. In the bottom half of the distribution, these falls have been substantial, wiping upwards of £30,000 of the average net worth of households across much of the bottom half.
> Half (51 per cent) of the 7.6 million families on low to middle incomes have no savings at all. Two-thirds (67 per cent) have less than a month's income in savings, leaving them vulnerable to small shocks. And many struggle to save or the longer term. Nearly three-quarters (71 per cent) of those on low to middle incomes have no pension or a frozen pension. Combined with the trends in home-ownership... many have in effect few or no assets on retirement.[7]

The fact that the Bank of England has kept interest rates so low is undoubtedly one factor in containing mortgage repayments to the extent that the mass repossession of private homes hasn't been seen on the scale we might have expected on the basis of previous recessions. But analysts have calculated that on conservative estimates an extra half a million – and perhaps as many as two million – people will find themselves in "debt peril", where an increase in interest rates will see over half their disposable income going to debt repayments:

On the most adverse, but still plausible, scenario looked at in the Resolution Foundation analysis the number of households in Britain who spend at least half their disposable income on repaying debts (and are therefore deemed to be in debt peril) could more than triple – from 600,000 in 2011 to 2 million by 2018. This could happen if interest rates were to rise to 5 per cent – two points higher than the current market expectation but still around typical long-term levels – and if growth in household income was weak and uneven (lagging behind GDP growth and more skewed towards higher than lower income households).

Even under a more optimistic scenario, in which interest rates do not rise above 3 per cent by 2018 and in which household incomes grow more strongly than the OBR has projected and are distributed relatively evenly across high to low income households, the number of families in debt peril would almost double – to 1.1 million.[8]

Struggling to keep afloat

With poverty already a reality for many families across the UK at the start of 2015, millions more have been only just keeping their heads above water. The Money Advice Service reckons that 8.8 million people (18% of the UK adult population) are "over-indebted" in the UK,[9] by which they mean having fallen at least three months behind on their bills over the last six months or having said that they feel their debts are a heavy burden. In cities such as Hull, Manchester and Liverpool, more than 40% of the adult population have been struggling with debts.[10] "Over-indebted" households certainly do not fall into the media stereotype of feckless scroungers – 58% are in work, and 48% own their own homes.[11] Women are said to represent 62% of those over-indebted,[12] partly as a result of the gender pay gap and the greater proportion of woman who are single parents. Debt-advice charity StepChange argue that, if anything, this understates the extent of the problem, claiming

> 15 million people [in Britain] are falling behind on bills and using credit to pay for essential costs, including almost 6 million people using credit to make it through until payday, and almost 3 million using credit to keep up with existing credit commitments.[13]

With real incomes having been squeezed, while the price of essential spending items has been increased, the lack of savings to fall back on means millions of people are finding that their personal finances are becoming increasingly exposed. A study of 18-64 year olds by Legal and General[14] found that the average working-age family is just eleven days from the breadline, at which point they would need the help of family, friends or welfare benefits to get by. Already families live in fear of major one-off costs like car repairs or vet's bills, let alone the prospect of losing their job.

Payday loans

Many people have been forced to turn to the payday loan industry – designed to provide easy-access unsecured lending to those with pressing needs for a source of short-term finance, i.e. to tide you over for the rest of the month until your next payday. The sector has grown rapidly over recent years, with companies like Wonga, QuickQuid and The Money Shop becoming familiar household names. The market was thought to be worth £900m in 2008-9 but by 2011-2 was thought to be by the Office of Fair Trading (OFT) to be worth up to £2bn,[15] and had reportedly reached £4.8bn in 2014.[16]

This growth was fuelled by increasingly lavish spending advertising campaigns. Ofcom reported a 64% year-on-year increase in payday loans advertising since 2008:

> In 2008 there were 12 million "impacts" (the total number of times an advert is seen by viewers) among adults for payday loans. By 2012 this figure had risen to 7.5 billion – an average of 152 payday loan adverts per viewer on TV last year. Children aged 4-15 saw 3 million payday loan TV adverts in 2008... By 2012, 596 million were seen by 4-15 year olds meaning the average child [in this age group] saw 70 payday loan adverts last year.[17]

Little wonder that Martin Lewis (of the Moneysavingexpert website) told a committee of MPs that 14% of parents of under-10s responding to online questionnaire when telling their child they couldn't have a particular toy "have had a payday loan quoted to borrow the money from", while 30% of children under 10 are said to be "joking about these slogans, and laughing and repeating the slogans of payday lenders".[18] Lewis warned MPs: "We are in danger of grooming a new generation towards this type of borrowing; if you think we have got problems now, you wait until 10 years' time".[19]

Normalising debt

It is not just the volume of adverts but their deliberately light-hearted and trivialising messages that have been serving to "normalise" the use of often inappropriate and high-cost forms of personal lending. Ads using cartoon characters emphasise how "quick and convenient" it is to take out a payday loan but rarely warn of the potential cost of failing to meet repayment deadlines or point people to independent debt advisors. Several judgements of the Advertising Standards Authority have found against payday loan advertisers such as the Cash Lady adverts featuring Kerry Katona, who appeared to suggest that a payday loan was preferable to borrowing from a high street bank.

Given that a standard credit card will allow you to borrow at 10-20% APR compared to 4,000-5,000% APR for many payday loans, this is misleading to say the least. Of course, if the debt is paid off over the intended duration (of up to a month) the annual percentage rate doesn't reflect the cost over the term of the loan. But since the loans have been not infrequently "rolled-over" from month to month, these extravagant rates are indeed leading people into spiralling debt problems. The OFT found that around 50% of revenues generated from payday loans come from customers who roll-over their initial debt rather than meet the original repayment terms.[20] In other words, the expectation that borrowers would end up paying usurious rates of interest has been built into the business model.

Bombarding the vulnerable

But perhaps worse than the volume of general advertising is the way that payday lenders regularly bombard people with existing debts with further unsolicited texts, emails and calls promoting the ease and availability of further short-term loans. Debt advice charity StepChange deals with clients who are often "at their lowest ebb" and "massively financially vulnerable". A third of its clients (who have average unsecured debts of around £16,000) have received such messages, with those who have been targeted receiving an average of 10 calls per week and some receiving dozens of calls. The legal loan sharks are targeting people in a vulnerable position, seeking to exploit their anxiety. Two StepChange clients recall their experience of the nuisance calls:

"When you're as desperate as I was, it's strangely comforting to know that there was money available no questions asked. The reality of course is that you're digging yourself deeper and deeper into a hole, and these companies know that."

"It started off slowly at maybe three or four calls a day but by the end of the week we're talking 40, 50 calls a day... even text messages, it was constant... I say 'I don't want any more debt' and they'll still try and they'll ring up and offer me all sorts. No matter how many times I say 'no I'm not interested' they'll just keep on ringing." [21]

The implication that loans are available "no questions asked" is also a clear breach of the lenders' duty to act responsibly, by checking to ensure the client is not burdening themselves with debts beyond their means. As Mike O'Connor, the charity's chief executive, commented,

> For those in financial difficulty, the offer of an easy, no-questions asked loan can seem like a financial lifeline. The reality is that it can be a financial noose around the neck of vulnerable people and their families.[22]

If you're struggling to pay back existing loans, the last thing you need is to be bombarded by encouragements to take out further loans and spiral even deeper into debt.

Spiralling debt

However, it's not just in soliciting for new business that the actions of the lenders amount to harassment and intimidation. Academics from Brighton University found that "irresponsible lending and harassing collection tactics" have "left thousands of people trapped in a spiral of debt and at risk of depression and even suicide".[23] StepChange reports that 74% of its clients said worry over debt was causing them to lose sleep and 43% reported that it was affecting their concentration at work.[24] The crisis and the austerity that has followed in its wake have pushed working people close to, and tragically sometimes even over, the edge.

One such tragic, though sadly not exceptional, case widely reported in the media was that of Ian Jordan, a 60 year old grandfather from Southampton, who committed suicide by overdosing on painkillers, having fallen into £20,000 debt to a number of payday loan firms after having his disability benefits cut and being out of work. Having taken out one payday loan in order to pay household bills, he reportedly began to find his debts spiralling out control. His phone reportedly received over a thousand text messages in the wake of his death including continued demands for payment, with the grieving family also being hassled to repay. One lender is believed to have refused to accept a copy of the death certificate. His daughter Samantha told the *Daily Mail*:

> Even after I told these companies about Dad's death, his phone was still receiving texts and calls demanding repayments — or offering him new loans. Then they started sending texts to my phone, offering me loans, too. At one point I had Dad's phone and mine bleeping and vibrating every five minutes with messages from these companies. It was enough to drive anyone mad.[25]

The Brighton University report found that such behaviour was endemic across the debt recovery industry, including but not restricted to the collection of payday loan debts:

> ... a considerable majority of the over-indebted find themselves party to distressing and persistent collection

tactics that frequently constituted abuse. Several of the key OFT debt collection guidelines concerning the ways in which debt collection employees interact with clients were ignored during their daily work.

The way in which debt collection was carried out was variously and routinely described as 'mental warfare', 'intimidating' and 'horrific'. It was suggested by more than one collector that there was an expectation that collectors would threaten clients in order to secure repayment.

Clients described being bullied, patronised and harassed and that nothing that they could say or do would alter these practices of brutality. Even when clients had organised an accepted payment plan with the institution that they owed money to, they were frequently contacted by collectors seeking to increase repayments.[26]

Fake legal threats

One notorious example of the depths to which some of these lenders are prepared to stoop was the Financial Conduct Authority's finding that Wonga had to repay £2.6 million for inventing fake firms of solicitors in order to send out intimidating 'legal' letters to customers, sometimes even adding extra charges to the client for the privilege of being issued with the bogus letters. MPs called for police to investigate, since the practice could have potentially broken the law on multiple grounds, from fraud to impersonating a solicitor, even blackmail.[27] But though the embarrassing episode caused damage to Wonga's "fun" PR image, it seems to have got off relatively lightly with a fine and a slap on the wrist.

The impact for those on the receiving end of such tactics can be brutal. As the Brighton University researchers found:

debt clients frequently felt humiliated, disconnected and entrapped and that the processes of debt collection outlined above had a clear impact on people's mental health. The harassment and the feeling of being uncontrollably entrapped in these practices of harassment related to experiences of despair, depression, suicidal ideation and what was frequently referred to as 'breakdown'. People talked of having no opportunity to escape from the pressure.[28]

Not only do the collectors fail to show any sense of human understanding or sympathy in dealing with people who have fallen into debt, they make no effort to point vulnerable people to sources of personal debt advice, or accept that other debts might take priority in terms of repayment (for instance where there is a chance of home repossession or having utilities cut off). Indeed, the pressure to take out new loans at unfavourable terms adds to their financial woes. While it might be one step removed from the criminal loan sharks "sending round the heavies" to recover debts, debt recovery practices of currently legal businesses are often similar in terms of the levels of psychological distress caused.

Left penniless

One practice frequently cited in criticism of the payday lenders' collection methods is the use of so-called Continuous Payment Authorities (CPAs). These are somewhat like Direct Debits but with fewer protections. Effectively it means the customer gives a company the right to use their debit card to make withdrawals at any time. The OFT issued guidance in response to complaints about the "aggressive" use of CPAs:

Lenders should not use CPA without the informed consent of the borrower or in ways that have not been agreed, and should always explain how CPA works and how it can be cancelled. Lenders should also not try to take payment where there is reason to believe there are insufficient funds in the account, nor should they continue using CPA for an unreasonable period after a scheduled payment was due.[29]

However, the reality remains that CPA's are flagrantly abused. The Citizens Advice Bureau reported that

one in three complaints about payday loans made to [them] were because of CPAs. Nine in ten payday loan customers who complain about the controversial payment method could have grounds for a complaint about unfair treatment:

▸ 9 in 10 could have grounds for a complaint to the Financial Ombudsman Service

▸ 1 in 5 were already in financial difficulty or on a debt management plan

▸ 1 in 6 had money taken without their authorisation

▸ 1 in 6 said that the payday lender used a CPA to take more money than they had originally agreed

▸ In some cases, bank accounts are completely drained, leaving people with no option but to borrow more to cover basic costs like food or rent, and face high overdraft fees and late payment charges if there isn't enough money to cover all payments.[30]

CPAs have left some people literally penniless and destitute. Alongside benefit sanctions, this was one of the key drivers of people having to turn to food banks, being put at risk of being made homeless or facing even greater problems with debt. CPAs mean that lenders who find that the debtor lacks the funds can make repeated attempts to raid the account – despite the clear evidence that the individual concerned is experiencing difficulties. The unpredictable nature of the withdrawals – particularly where incomes are irregular, such as for people on zero-hours contracts – can have a devastating impact, and push people into taking out further payday loans just to get by.

Weak reforms

After a great deal of campaigning by charities, trade unions and MPs, the Financial Conduct Authority announced that from January 2015 there will be stricter regulation of the sector – with a cap of 0.8% interest per day, a cap on default charges of £15, a limit of two "roll-overs" and the total cost of the loan limited to double the original value. Action has been too slow in coming, and critics of the industry such as Labour MP Stella Creasy have warned that payday lenders are trying to evade the regulations (which in any case would only reduce the value of the average loan by £1), by "altering the terms of the loans they offer in an apparent attempt to circumvent definitions of short-term credit, moving from 1000s% APR over a matter of weeks to 100s% over 6 months or longer, or offering to 'top-up' loans rather than offer a new loan each time".[31]

Creasy concludes that even with the regulations in place, British consumers will be less well protected than their counterparts in Japan or most of the United States and Canada. The regulations will do little to alter the fundamental business model, or tackle the issue of new loans being offered to people already struggling with multiple debts. To really tackle the problem we would need a comprehensive package of measures addressing the financial difficulties which often lay behind the demand for sort-term lending at sky-high rates of interest.

The Change we need

▶ Alleviate financial pressures by boosting incomes, reversing the squeeze of the proportion of national income going to wages and protecting the value of benefits while ending the subsidy to employers paying low wages or landlords hiking up the rent (see Housing chapter)

▶ Introduce the measures contained in Paul Blomfield MP's Private Members Bill on "High Cost Credit" including:

> ▶ Tighter regulations on payday loans advertising before the watershed, and on unsolicited email, texts and phone messages

> ▶ Require payday lenders to point actual and potential customers to debt advice lines, and to pay a proportion of their profits towards funding these services

> ▶ A requirement to introduce a repayment plan and suspend further enforcement action and charges where a debt advice agency contacts a payday lender on a client's behalf following a default

> ▶ Compel high street banks to introduce a protected minimum balance on current accounts which would mean CPA or other payments could not leave people with nothing in their accounts

> ▶ Promote wider access to credit unions via opening up the Post Office network

> ▶ Introduce "real-time" checking of existing client debts to prevent irresponsible lending

> ▶ Investigate options for publicly owned banks to take over and restructure unsecured consumer debts, writing off those elements relating to misleading sales, unfair charges or instances of non-compliance with industry codes of practice.

6

Cost of Caring for your Family

Raising a family is expensive. To bring-up one child can cost nearly a quarter of a million pounds. Research by the Centre for Economic and Business Research (CEBR) for insurance company LV estimates that the cost of raising a child to the age of 21 (including helping them fund their way through higher education) now stands at over £227,000, up from £140,398 when the series began in 2003, a colossal 62% increase.[1] NatWest argues this is an underestimate, and that raising a child from birth to 17 years old in fact costs an average of £307,083![2]

By the time a baby reaches its first birthday it will have cost an average of £11,025, once baby clothes, accessories, cots, prams, painting and decorating a nursery, babysitting and reduced wages from maternity and paternity leave are taken into account.[3] Another study argued that expectant parents need a minimum of £5,464 in the bank before starting a family to pay for these early costs, but less than one in four (23 per cent) have been able to save enough for such a "baby buffer" before starting a family.[4] Given the squeeze in the value of real wages, rising costs of essential goods and difficulty saving for a deposit on a house, the likelihood is that it will only get further out of reach for new parents. Little wonder that more than half will look to their own parents for financial help in the early weeks of a baby's life.[5]

The cost of childcare

But the bad news is that it only gets more costly from there on in. The cost of pre-school nursery care for toddlers has been rising sharply. The Family and Daycare Trust calculate that "over the last five years childcare costs have risen 27 per cent – meaning parents pay £1,214 more in 2014 than they did in 2009".[6] This cost is increasing more than five times faster than pay. With child benefits and tax credits also falling in relation to inflation, this additional burden further squeezes a working family's income. The survey shows that "the cost of sending a child under two to nursery part-time (25 hours) is now £109.89 per week in Britain or £5,710 per year. For a family with two children in full-time childcare, the yearly bill is £11,703. This makes childcare costs 62 per cent higher than the cost of the average mortgage for a family home".[7] This burden falls particularly heavily on women and single parents in particular. Polling shows that 7 out of 10 women are put off returning to work by the cost of childcare.[8] Parents working part-time on average wages typically find themselves working from Monday through to Thursday just to cover their childcare costs.

Even though the UK is one of the eight richest countries in the world (measured by nominal GDP),[9] more than one in four children grows up in poverty, that means a total of around 3.5 million.[10] Of these, two thirds are in families with at least one parent in work. Current projections show that by 2020, 4.7 million children in the UK will live in poverty.[11] Children in poverty grow up missing out on what other children can take for granted – getting to go on a school trip, getting enough pocket money to enjoy a social life, or getting away for a week's holiday. There is abundant evidence that children living in poverty suffer in terms of educational and health indicators.

Early years support is vital in giving children the best possible start in life, but the least well-off areas have often suffered from a lack of quality local services. The national network of around 4,000 Sure Start centres established by the last Labour government provided an essential lifeline to parents, offering a range of services from childcare to parenting, health and education support and help back into work. The Sure Start centres were also effectively placed to help the hardest-to-reach, most deprived families who were for the first time entitled to receive free, publicly provided weekly pre-school care and support.

Sadly, despite their election promises, Sure Start has been badly hit by the coalition's austerity cuts. There are now 578 fewer Sure Start centres (which have been closing at the rate of approximately three every week since 2010) and there are 35,000 fewer childcare places, even though the number of under-4s has risen by 125,000. It doesn't take a genius to work out what the effect this is having. More than half of all local authorities (51%) did not have enough childcare places for working parents, while only one in four (25%) had enough childcare for disabled children.[12] "Over 30,000 of England's poorest two-year-olds miss out on free nursery education...[which represents] over one quarter (26 per cent) of this cohort" and "there are 37 local authorities where less than 60 per cent of eligible two-year-olds had been placed".[13]

But it's not just pre-school childcare that has been hit under Cameron and Clegg. Funding for schools to provide breakfast and after-school clubs, vital for parents working full-time hours with school-age children, was no longer ring-fenced. Before 2010, 99% of schools provided access to such services. But with the savage cuts to their budgets, more than a third of local authorities have reported that this has been scaled back or scrapped. Costs have also risen, with the average after-school club now costing nearly £1,830 a year, or nearly £50 per week.[14] Childcare during the school holidays is even thinner on the ground, with only

27% of English local authorities and 6% of those in Wales having enough childcare provisions at these times. The Family and Childcare Trust reported that "35% of parents found it difficult to find holiday childcare they could afford: 25% of parents had been forced to cut their hours, 17% said they had taken days off sick and 12% of parents had given up a job".[15] Finding adequate provision is harder still for disabled children or in rural areas.

The coalition's record on childcare has intensified the effect of rising costs on working parents on low incomes, since it has have failed to uprate the childcare component of working tax credits in line with the massive rise in prices since 2005. Its policies are based on a shift away from government guarantees of free childcare entitlements towards a more "demand" based approach, making childcare payments tax-free and leaving individuals to shop around for services as they feel appropriate. This has been described by the IPPR as "regressive, skewed towards benefiting higher income families",[16] since it offers nothing to the poorest parents who fall below the income tax threshold, yet will offer huge savings for the wealthier who pay for expensive care options. As they comment:

> The government has not proposed how they would regulate the market, nor control prices, making a demand led strategy unstable despite significant investment. It is clear that more radical reforms are needed as affordability and quality will remain critical. Supply-funded systems that offer direct childcare provision or direct payments to childcare providers tend to be more effective at achieving lower net childcare costs compared to their total expenditure as well as a focus on high quality provision. Many of these systems also cap costs for parents to ensure fairness. Early year's provision is not a commodity that should be largely provided and regulated by market

forces. The current direction of travel suggests that costs for parents will continue to spiral despite government investment.[17]

With the government pursuing an approach that is costly, unfair and ineffective, it is unlikely that the costs will start to fall anytime soon.

Food, clothes and Father Christmas

Of course, bringing up children involves costs other than childcare. There's feeding them, for one thing. The CEBR study estimates that parents will spend an average of nearly £20,000 per child on food and drink by the time they reach 21.[18] With the cost of essential foodstuffs having risen sharply over recent years just finding the money to put food on the table has become a stretch for thousands. The "Below the Breadline" report produced by charities providing for the food poor in Britain suggests that "UK food prices have increased by 43.5 per cent in the eight years to July 2013".[19] The greater proportion of income going towards food costs, during a period of falling real wages and benefit cuts, has seen food bank charity the Trussell Trust report the number of clients visiting their food banks has more than doubled inside 12 months.[20] Then there's clothing, now estimated to cost the average parent over £10,000 per child up to 21.

Meeting the needs of the child is just part of the bill. Adverts and marketing messages are encouraging young consumers to demand more and more. These 'promotions' also impose non-monetary costs like health problems. This includes anorexia, the result of low self-esteem arising from the commercial promotion of unrealistic body images. Of even more concern is obesity, encouraged by advertisements featuring junk food and sugar laden sweets.

One study[21] showed that parents typically spend an average of £460 per year on things they did not need, after being pestered for items seen on television or on display in stores. Sweets, snacks and junk food leading the way, but also for items less obviously attractive for children including DIY tools (13%) and cleaning products (8%).

Christmas puts a special pressure on the budgets of parents, so anxious not to disappoint that they are willing to go into debt to buy the latest gifts so their kids do not feel left out. The average list to Father Christmas now comes in at an average of £880[22] – expensive gadgets like iPods, iPads and iPhones increasingly crop up alongside footballs, bikes or dolls. 57% of kids told researchers that they get their ideas from watching adverts. Given this added pressure to have the latest hi-tech games console or the right brand of trainers, hard-pressed parents are taking on more debt in order not to disappoint on the big day.

But children also need financial support a long time after they stop believing in Santa. According to Office of National Statistics figures, 3.3 million young adults (aged between 20-34) still live with their parents.[23] This is the result of a variety of factors, from the impact of youth unemployment during the recession to the long-term shortage in housing supply driving up prices and rents. As we saw in the Great Pay Robbery booklet, it now takes a two-earner couple eleven years to find enough for a deposit in London, while a single earner would take over a decade to earn enough to become a first-time buyer in 76% of local authority areas across the UK.[24] Many of those who do get a foot on the housing ladder have been able to turn to the "bank of Mum and Dad" - with parents contributing £2 billion a year to help their children become homeowners. But if parents can't afford to shoulder a financial burden, they are increasingly seeing their children living at home into their thirties. Relationship guidance charity Relate reports that this is "putting pressure on parents who had expected their children to move out when they went into higher education... Couples who had held on for the sake of the children find that they are holding on for longer."[25]

Tuition fees and textbooks

Finance is also a major potential barrier for young people wanting to go into higher education, not least since the coalition government trebled university tuition fees. Research from the Sutton Trust shows that the average student will now have to face in excess of £44,000 debt from going through HE, and face making repayments into their 40s and 50s.[26] While this debt burden might remain notional in the first instance, with those on the lowest incomes not having to make repayments, those who go into jobs like teaching will "have to find up to £2,500 extra a year to service loans at a time when their children are still at school, and family and mortgage costs are at their most pressing".[27] The prospect of having this albatross around your neck for most of your working life is understandably something that would make you think twice about continuing in education at all.

But long before the question of loan repayment kicks in, students have to consider far more than the cost of their tuition fees, including the cost of textbooks, accommodation fees, travel and other day-to-day living costs, which mount up quickly. The cost of the cheapest university digs increased by an average of 11% over the period 2011 -2014,[28] further raising the barriers to entry for the poorest students. Around two thirds of students are now subsidising themselves by working part-time alongside their studies,[29] frequently in places such as fast food restaurants or bars where they are more likely to be exploited on zero-hours contracts. In this environment it is no surprise that 237,000 students now choose to keep costs down by continuing to live with their parents whilst studying at university. As with childcare, as universal entitlements have come under attack, the system is returning to one of privilege for those who can afford it. For those students whose parents are either unable or unwilling to cushion the blow by helping out financially or keeping a roof over their heads, higher education looks increasingly unaffordable.

Tying the knot

The costs of parenting do not even end when they've fled the nest. With the average wedding now costing in excess of £18,000[30] it's likely you'll be asked for help here too, if not with the cost of the honeymoon (on average £3,582), or the rings (£1,856) then perhaps with the wedding dress (£1,098), the venue (£2,164), the catering (£2,770), the flowers, decoration and cake (£728), or the photographer (£876).[31] That's before we get to kitting out any bridesmaids, groomsmen or pageboys.

Then, given the lack of affordable childcare we have discussed, grandparents are increasingly called upon to step into the breach. Of course, spending time with their grandkids might not seem like a chore, but being permanently required for regular unpaid shifts is something else. It is estimated that the generosity of grandparents with their time relieves the state over around £8 billion in spending every year. However, polling evidence suggests that nearly 2 million grandparents (14%) "have cut their working hours, given up jobs, or taken annual or sick leave to care for their grandchildren."[32] Together with those parents, usually mothers, who find that the lack of affordable childcare options means it's not worthwhile to go out to work, the impact of volunteers meeting needs with unpaid work is detrimental to the overall economy.

The crisis in care

But childcare is just one part of an overall crisis in care services, including help for elderly, sick and disabled adults who need help with everyday tasks in order to live independent lives. The coalition will have forced £20 billion in cuts and "efficiency savings" from the budgets of local councils by 2015, which has produced a devastating effect on the range and quality of local services provided at a time when demand is growing steeply. Adult care services have been particularly affected, with care increasingly restricted to those deemed eligible for substantial and critical care support. Charges have been introduced for some services formerly available for free, and other services have been withdrawn altogether. The *Guardian* reported that "over a quarter of a million older people have lost their state-funded help with carrying out everyday activities such as bathing, dressing and eating".[33]

Many of those who do continue to receive visits find that they are given assistance for no longer than 15 minutes. The Leonard Cheshire Disability charity has indicated that "63 local authorities pointed to a 15% rise in such visits in the last five years" and that "in some councils more than 75% of care visits were carried out in less than 15 minutes."[34] This is often manifestly inadequate to meet the multiple daily needs of elderly or disabled people.

These attacks on the care services available to adults mean the burden is again increasingly falling on unpaid family members or neighbours willing to provide help, or else needs are going unmet, at the same time as benefit entitlements are being withdrawn or questioned (see Great Pay Robbery). Far from helping carers and rewarding them for their immense contribution to helping vulnerable people live independent lives, the coalition has seen fit to leave even more unpaid work at their door.

Finally, as we live longer, more of us are likely to end our lives in residential or nursing care homes. Here, too, the cost of a room is said to have rocketed by 9.3% in the two years to 2013, and now represents more than double the average pensioner's income, meaning that pensioners are forced to eat more deeply into any savings they might have.[35] However, it's not just the cost of a care home that concerns most of us but the quality of the care received. Keeping costs down by employing unsuitable staff on exploitative zero-hours contracts is hardly a recipe for better care. With the private sector running care homes, the danger is that there is more concern for the balance sheet than with providing adequate care for the residents.

The collapse of the Southern Cross group in 2011 saw shareholders of US private equity concern Blackstone make a killing by leaving the company seriously over-leveraged – and 31,000 residents in 752 homes facing the wrench of being forced to move if they company went bust. Only the intervention of a taxpayer bailout protected the elderly residents. Clearly care was not at the top of the company's priorities, with a coroner's verdict describing the company's Orchid View home near Crawley as "mismanaged and understaffed" and riddled with "institutional abuse".[36] It's not what we would wish for ourselves or our loved ones, but sadly it does not appear to be an exceptional case.

The change we need

▶ Introduce free universal pre-school childcare
▶ Reinvest in Sure Start centres to offer quality early years provision to all
▶ Reverse benefit cuts and tax wealth to eradicate child poverty
▶ Ring-fence funding for every school to provide affordable breakfast and after-school clubs

▸ Curb commercial advertising during children's TV
▸ Restore full maintenance grants for higher education students including the cost of tuition
▸ Restore adult social care budgets to pre-2010 levels, reinstate benefit entitlements and boost caring allowances
▸ Properly integrate social care, health care and mental health services into a single coherent and properly funded national system based on public ownership and control of resources, not market competition
▸ Extend the Scottish government's offer of free personal care for the elderly to England, Wales and Northern Ireland
▸ Boost the pay, conditions and training of residential care workers, and prevent homes from being taken over by asset-strippers, speculators and profiteers.

7

Cost of Energy

Electricity is a basic everyday essential that every household needs; most need Gas as well. Without the energy they supply we would be without heating, hot water and functioning domestic appliances. These are bills we must pay, but why must we pay through the nose? The basic infrastructure that provides energy to our homes is the same: the network of gas pipes and the national electricity grid. This used to be held in public ownership and run for the common public good, a sensible arrangement given that energy is not just any commodity but a key strategic industry on which everyone depends.

But in the 1980s, the Thatcher government began to pursue the ideologically-driven privatisation of the energy industry, putting profiteering private companies in charge of managing both the energy infrastructure and the domestic supply of gas and electricity to our homes. This also set in train the transfer of public assets in the energy generation sector into the hands of private shareholders.

Botched sell-off

By no means was this in the interest of the public finances. For instance, as a result of the botched privatisation, British Energy (a company whose assets included key nuclear power stations) ran into serious financial difficulties, requiring the government to step in with £3 billion support, to enable the company to be restructured under government control.[1] Once the public purse had absorbed the costs, the more commercially attractive bits were floated back on to the market. Eventually in 2006 it passed back into the hands of EDF Energy (which is, ironically, owned predominantly by the French state).

"Big six" dominate

Such privatisations have meant that the energy sector is "vertically integrated", in other words that the same companies responsible for generating energy are also responsible for buying that energy in order to supply it for domestic consumption. The market for both generation and supply is overwhelmingly dominated by the same "big six" energy companies – British Gas (part of the Centrica group); Npower (part of German energy giant RWE); SSE (formed by the merger of Scottish Hydro and Southern Electric); Scottish Power (owned by Spanish giant Iberdrola); E.ON (formerly Powergen before it was swallowed up by the German E.ON group); and EDF. These six companies are responsible for 95% of all UK household gas and electricity.

Punishing loyalty

The picture is all the more alarming when it comes to the near-monopoly power single companies hold in particular regions. Far from privatisation having opened up a competitive market that would force companies to be more efficient, as its advocates promised, in fact the majority of consumers have stuck with the majority local provider from the days of monopoly ownership.

An average of 70 per cent of households across all regions use the same electricity supplier, with the proportion rising to 85 per cent in some areas, undermining claims by the government and Ofgem, the regulator, that the energy market is operating competitively. Data from the Department for Energy and Climate Change (DECC) revealed that customers who have stayed with their old electricity supplier are paying more than those who have switched. DECC analysis shows that these "home suppliers" charge an average of £31 a year more than non-home suppliers for electricity – in effect placing a premium on loyalty. The largest five electricity suppliers dominate the regions they inherited from utility boards more than two decades ago, while British Gas still retains the largest share of the retail gas market nationwide. This is despite consumers being encouraged by price comparison websites to shop around for the cheapest supplier.[2]

Confusing tariffs

Consumers do not want to have to navigate a vast amount of complex data comparing rival companies' tariffs when even experts find difficulty in deciding which one would represent best value for money over the long term. Even if you manage to identify a tariff that appears to offer savings, the hassle of swapping providers (stopping and starting direct debits, choosing billing options etc.) means that few people want to change providers more than once in a blue moon. Most people just want a reliable service with minimum fuss which does not leave them feeling ripped off. Instead, private companies are punishing consumers for their loyalty, and failing to warn them even if their existing tariff is totally unsuitable.

Soaring prices

Whatever the tariff and the provider, most people have been seeing their gas and electric bills rise substantially over recent years, an effect that is all the more pronounced, when we take into account falling real incomes over the same period. According to the Department for Energy and Climate Change:

> the average prices of gas and electricity paid by UK households had risen by around 18% and 9% (in real terms), respectively between 2010 and 2013, and by around 41% and 20% (in real terms), respectively, between 2007 and 2013.[3]

As one energy price comparison site points out, "the average household energy bill is now an eye-watering £1,265 a year – £53 more than a year ago and an astonishing £793 or 168% higher than in 2004".[4]

After the 2013 price hikes, it is estimated that 14% of households are now in debt to their energy supplier, amounting to some £464 million. Consumer group *Which?* told MPs that "domestic energy prices were consistently either the highest or second highest concern, [and] up to 40% of consumers had used savings or credit to pay for their domestic energy".[5] Citizens Advice report that, with gas and electricity bills having risen around eight times as fast as incomes,

> the impact energy price rises are having on people's ability to have a decent standard of living is causing grave concerns... Bureaux often see clients who are on the brink of financial despair. Parents often face tough choices between putting the heating on, clothing their children and feeding the family.[6]

Fuel poverty

Analysts estimate that in early 2014 there were 6.59 million households in fuel poverty in the UK,[7] up from 4.45 million in

2011, as measured by the traditional definition of fuel poverty according to *Which?* a household

> needs to spend more than 10% of its income on fuel to maintain a satisfactory heating regime. This is considered to be 21C for the main living area and 18C for other occupied rooms during daytime hours. Besides space heating, fuel costs also include spending on energy for water heating, lights and appliances and cooking.[8]

This is not a measure of what households actually spend on heating, but of their needs in relation to their income, the price of energy and the energy efficiency of their homes. Fuel poverty particularly affects elderly and disabled people, infants and those with long-term sickness.

Vulnerable groups often need to use more energy because they spend more time at home, require heating during the night or over summer months for health reasons, and have greater laundry costs.[9] Taken together with rising prices, this can mean fuel poverty exacerbates already distressing circumstances. Scandalously, for example, 20% of people living with cancer told Macmillan that they have had to turn the heating off over winter due to money worries.[10]

The problem of fuel poverty is compounded by the fact that low income households are more likely to experience poor housing conditions, and face living in properties that suffer from damp and poor insulation. In comparison to more modern energy-efficient homes, these properties require greater energy usage to bring the home to a comfortable temperature. A home built in 1960 loses three times more heat than one built today.[11] The UK has the oldest housing stock in Europe,[12] which is another reason why Britain has a higher incidence of fuel poverty than countries such as Sweden, despite Sweden's colder climate.

Government inaction

Even though the British government now has a statutory duty to do everything "reasonable practicable" to eliminate fuel poverty by 2016, there is no sign of this target being met. Indeed, Prof John Hills, who was commissioned by the government to report on fuel poverty, estimated that 8.5 million people will be unable afford their energy bills by 2016. But far from helping, in some respects the coalition government took us backwards, by failing to address spiralling energy costs while refusing new claimants access to schemes like Warm Front, which helped poor and vulnerable people struggling with fuel bills to make their homes more energy efficient. This is an outrage given that according to World Health Organisation estimates 30-50% of excess winter deaths can be attributed to cold indoor temperatures. In the UK around 60 people a day – 7,800 a year – die because they are unable to heat their homes properly.[13]

Pre-pay meters punish the poorest

Some of the poorest households are paying up to £300 a year[14] more for their energy than more affluent consumers, since the energy companies typically charge more per unit of energy bought via pre-paid meters than for tariffs based on payment via direct debit or traditional credit. Similarly, those who are already in debt are more likely to find themselves trapped into paying via such meters, having to put up with the inconvenience and the danger of finding themselves without power. Pre-payment meters also do nothing to enable families to spread the burden of heating costs throughout the year rather than facing a particular burden during the cold winter months.

Similarly, they can also be subject to standing charges, meaning that consumers not only pay more for the energy they use, but also for the dubious privilege of having their power supply regulated by pre-pay meter in the first place! For example, for every £10 of energy credit bought on SSE pre-payment cards, £1.92 goes into standing charges. Scotland's *Daily Record* newspaper calls it a "stealth charge" on 900,000 of the company's poorest customers. Granddad-of-two Dennis told the reporter that he had to live on £140 a week of benefits and tried to spend no more than £20 on gas: "These energy companies have no idea how a few pounds a week can have a big impact on people's lives. Either that, or they just do not care".[15]

Billions in profit

While families across the country have been plunged into despair over the prospects of keeping warm, the fat cat bosses at the top of the big energy companies have been doing very nicely. Consumer Focus told MPs that "the pre-tax and investment UK profits of the big six energy companies increased by 36% between 2008 and 2011, from £6.67 billion to £9.09 billion",[16] although supply of energy to domestic properties represents only one dimension, with a sizeable chunk of these profits coming from the generation and trading of energy. It is no by means straightforward to analyse and compare the profit margins of each aspect of a company's activity – and despite Ofgem's attempts to require transparency in the publication of financial statements, the Energy and Climate Change Select Committee found that:

> Despite huge turnovers, and in some cases large profits, the six largest energy companies have made significantly different levels of profit and loss between the supply and generation parts of their business. The actual level of profit in, for example, the energy supply arm is therefore difficult to establish... We remain concerned that efforts are falling

far short of what is required to improve transparency, increase competition and enhance consumer trust.[17]

Energy company bosses have been quick to cite the "complexity" of the industry as a reason for failing to adequately account for recent price rises. But consumers rightly suspect that the profit from their rising energy bill is being trousered by wealthy shareholders. Take E.ON, which raised its bills by around 9% at the start of 2013[18] and then posted a profit rise on the supply of energy to UK homes of 26%,[19] or Centrica (owner of British Gas), which saw its profits rise 9% to £1.58bn for the period to June last year after having put up its average dual-fuel bill by over 9%. Was this pure coincidence?

Of course this is not to deny that costs of generation have been increasing. Part of the problem is the over-reliance on increasingly depleted stores of fossil fuels, which are becoming progressively harder to extract. Aside from this, we cannot afford the damage to the climate which would follow from any failure to meet carbon emissions targets. As campaigners point out:

Once extraction, which is becoming increasingly energy intensive, and transportation are taken into account, gas isn't that much cleaner than coal. The government's independent climate advisers, the Committee on Climate Change (CCC), have stated that the low carbon grid of 2030 should produce no more than 50g of CO_2 for every kilowatt hour of electricity generated. Gas produces 350g CO_2 for every kilowatt hour at the point of generation.[20]

Any energy mix which depends upon expensive and risky technologies such as hydraulic fracturing ("fracking") of shale gas deposits threatens further escalating costs – and environmental damage. Similarly, new nuclear power plants are likely to require billions in public subsidy, with the new Hinckley Point C plant in Somerset alone costing a staggering £24.5 billion to build. As part of the deal brokered by the government, the British taxpayer will be locked into paying double the current wholesale price per unit of energy for the next 35 years. For this, EDF gets to pocket 40% of all profits over and above the 13.5% return on capital guaranteed in the contract. Greenpeace called it a "world record sell out to the nuclear industry at the expense of the taxpayer and the environment". It's hard to disagree. Former Number 10 policy advisor Nick Butler commented in a blog for the *Financial Times*, "The deal will go down in history, alongside the privatisation of the Royal Mail, as an example of the inability of the British government – ministers and civil servants alike – to negotiate complex commercial deals". We will be left paying the price.

Long-term upwards pressure on bills

The National Audit Office has projected that the energy infrastructure of the UK requires £176 billion of investment in order to replace ageing assets, meet policy commitments on climate and cope with the needs of a growing population. The NAO report states bluntly what this is likely to mean:

> High levels of expected investment in new infrastructure mean... bills may rise significantly. Consumers will pay for the infrastructure itself, along with the costs of maintaining and operating the infrastructure. Future bills will also be influenced by other factors, such as changes in world energy prices and initiatives to help consumers use less energy and water. The Department of Energy and Climate Change's central projection is for an 18% increase in energy bills in real terms by 2030.[21]

Structural pressures mean that already sky-high bills are likely to climb higher over the coming years unless we take a radically different approach.

Resetting the market?

As Leader of the Opposition, Ed Miliband talked of "resetting the energy market" and helping out hard-pressed consumers with a two-year energy price freeze opening up an important debate on how working people are being ripped-off at the hands of the energy bosses. It is no surprise that the promise of some relief from massive increases in fuel bills would receive a warm welcome given the present cost of living crisis. In response, Centrica's chief executive Sam Laidlaw – who received a package of pay and benefits of £2.2 million in 2013,[22] on top of nearly £4.3m the previous year[23] – chose to blackmail the public with the threat that this policy would see a return to blackouts and threatening to pull the plug on investment. However, despite the initial cry of alarm from the fat cats, the big companies started to reconcile themselves to Miliband's fairly modest set of proposals. SSE, for example, voluntarily announced a price freeze to 2016.

Nevertheless, there are obvious limitations to Labour's willingness to tackle the power of the energy companies. A price freeze can be anticipated by front-loading rises to bills before the freeze kicks in, or storing up increases until after 2016. Similarly, shareholders can look to protect their profit margins by slackening levels of investment. Even former Tory PM Sir John Major, recognising that Miliband's price freeze would do little to claw back the mega-profits that energy firms have extorted from the taxpayer, proposed a windfall tax on their excess profits. There is a case for such a tax, but this still wouldn't address the ongoing structural flaws in the energy market. A positive move could be separating generation, trading and supply, making the reporting of profits genuinely transparent and replacing the failed regulator Ofgem.

Bolder action needed

But polling evidence suggests the public would be bolder still. Why should shareholders of multinational companies cream off profits from providing energy, when the industry could be brought back under public ownership and run in the common public interest? Why shouldn't billions in profits be re-invested in keeping energy bills down via energy efficiency programmes to make a warm home affordable to all? Instead of short-sighted investment in fossil fuels, a publicly owned energy industry could invest in renewables and green technologies which would – over the medium term – begin to deliver a de-carbonised, affordable and sustainable future. A YouGov poll last year saw 68% of respondents support the idea the energy companies should be in the public sector, including even a majority (52%) of Tory voters![24]

We would not need to return to a bureaucratic, top-down model of state ownership where workers and consumers are excluded from remote structures of decision-making. An energy revolution could allow local community energy co-operatives to contribute to a genuine mix of renewable energies helping to break reliance on fossil fuels.

The change we need

▶ Bring the energy companies back into public ownership – keep bills down, invest for the future and run utilities for the common good

▶ Expand energy-efficiency programmes to insulate homes, with targeted support for the least well off

▶ Pre-payment meters only installed on request, with no unfair pricing and charges

▶ Work with credit unions and local authorities to provide low-cost credit for the fuel poor
▶ Break from the dependence on fossil fuels – invest in renewable energies such as wind, solar, and wave
▶ Encourage local community energy co-operatives
▶ No to fracking.

8

Cost of Transport

Transport has been a key ingredient in the cost of living crisis. Travel by public transport is becoming unaffordable for those on modest incomes. Over a period when real wages have been held down, rail prices have gone up by an eye-watering 25% since the 2010 general election, while average nominal earnings rose by just 10.7% over the same period.

The coalition scrapped the Retail Price Index (RPI) measure of inflation for calculating pay rises, pensions and benefits in favour of the less generous Consumer Price Index (CPI). However when it comes to calculating rises in the cost of rail fares, the benchmark is still RPI, in 2014 fares increased by an average of 2.2% and by 2.5% for peak fares, nearly twice the rate of CPI inflation (1.3%), which itself is still outstripping many workers' pay settlements.[1]

Rocketing fares

Since the privatisation of the rail network fares have risen on average by 22% in real terms,[2] and the price of walk-on fares has risen in some instances by as much as 245%.[3] With an eye on the General Election, George Osborne chose to freeze the additional "flex" rule that would otherwise have seen some fares rises by 5.6%, but he did not ruled out letting train companies whack up peak fares again in future years.

People relying on rail services to get to their workplaces are feeling the pinch acutely, with commuters in Britain typically spending more than 14% of their income on fares, compared to less than 5% in Germany, Italy, Spain and France.[4] In 2015 a season ticket from Reading to London, for example, will cost a whopping £4,325, following an increase of £147, and it will be £3,203 from Plymouth to Exeter St Davids. Similarly, to the anger of passengers who depend on its services, Northern Rail placed restrictions on early evening services, which meant they are now subject to expensive peak-time fares. Some fares were increased by over 100%. For low paid and part-time workers, not able to take advantage of season ticket offers due to changing shift patterns, this is a particularly heavy blow.

Overcrowding

Where is all this extra revenue going? If it was all invested in producing a faster, safer, more reliable, less overcrowded rail network then rail passengers might be open to paying a little extra. However, the evidence suggests that the pain far exceeds any gains, with less than half of respondents to the latest Passenger Focus survey (45%) feeling that train travel offers overall value for money.[5]

Many commuters are paying thousands every year without even the luxury of a seat for their journeys to show for it. Government figures show that over 100,000 people every day have to stand on their commuter journeys into London,[6] with 48% of passengers on London Overground services having to stand in the morning rush-hour. It's not only in the capital where passengers face overcrowded conditions. The lowest ranked train operating company in customer satisfaction ratings last year was First Transpennine Express, with just 58% of respondents judging their journey satisfactory in terms of space on the train.[7]

Subsidising failure

With passengers also complaining about ageing rolling stock, delays, cancellations and over-running engineering works, it is hardly any wonder that people do not feel they've been getting value for money. Rocketing fares are not the only way in which the travelling public has been ripped off. The nation continue to subsidise the private rail operators to the tune of over £4 billion a year.[8] Privatised railways have become a significantly greater drain on the public purse than the nationalised service was, with subsidies having risen by in excess of 66% compared to those enjoyed in the final year of British Rail's existence.[9]

However, even this underestimates the real level of subsidy enjoyed by private operators, since Network Rail (which has finally been brought back into public ownership, after being set up as a not-for-profit company due to the debacle of the profiteering Railtrack going into administration) has been charging just £1.59 billion to allow private companies access to the track, compared to £3.18 billion formerly charged by Railtrack. This hidden subsidy, on top of the billions openly paid to the private companies, has allowed them to protect their profits and direct 90% of them to shareholders in the forms of dividends, £200 million in 2013.[10]

Costly privatisation

The bottom line is that the myth that was peddled – that private competition would increase efficiency on our railways – has turned out to be utterly untrue, having in fact produced the opposite effect. Even Sir Roy McNulty, commissioned by the government to justify austerity-driven cuts, was forced to admit that

the industry has problems in terms of efficiency and costs ... among the principal barriers are fragmentation of structures and interfaces ... ineffective and misaligned incentives, a franchising system that does not encourage cost reduction sufficiently, management approaches ... and a railway culture which is not conducive to the partnership and continuous improvement approaches required for effective cost reduction.[11]

In other words, privatisation has fragmented the system such that the company running the track, the train operating companies running passenger services and the companies leasing them the rolling stock (ROSCOs) all have different and sometimes clashing interests. Inevitably, the multiple interfaces between these different sub-units leads to inefficiency and greater costs, before we even get to the multiplied opportunities for shareholders to leech from the system in the form of their dividends.

The franchising system inevitably means that rival operators each have to line up a massive army of accountants, consultants, lawyers and marketing specialists in order to formulate competitive bids, while another army of civil servants is required to analyse and compare them. The fiasco of the collapse of the franchising round on the West Coast line alone is judged to have cost us all at least £50 million, the real figure could be "very much larger.[12] Even where the process does not fail so spectacularly, it is an inherently wasteful and inefficient use of resources by organisations that rely on such lavish subsidies from taxation and passengers.

In fact the views of passengers do not count for very much when deciding if a private company's performance is adequate. Southeastern commuters recorded the lowest overall satisfaction ratings of all the 23 franchise operators, with just 30% regarding them as offering value for money. However, the government decided this was still enough to merit rewarding them with an extension of their franchise until the middle of 2018 without even considering the benefits of improving the service under public ownership.

Franchising chaos

The franchising system also understandably limits the horizons of the rival operators, who are reluctant to take long-term strategic investment plans from which they are not certain to benefit. The argument that privatisation transfers the risk from the public sector to the private sector is another obvious lie. In fact, academic experts have calculated that the "return on capital" (the level of profitability relative to the outlay a company has "risked") in the rail industry is a mammoth 147%, indicating that companies are making a great deal of profit in return for risking a small level of investment.[13]

In effect the risk of private sector failure remains with the taxpayer, as with the collapse of Railtrack, which means that the privatised rail network is effectively a licence for the rich shareholder to print money. Public sector operators like Directly Operated Railways (DOR), which rode to the rescue to provide passenger services on the East Coast main line when National Express pulled the plug on its franchise, not only displayed a better level of performance but also returned £208m back to public funds.[14] But rather than allow this to become a precedent for the rest of the network, the government was ideologically insistent that it must be handed back to the private sector. Shareholders in Stagecoach and Virgin, the joint private consortium awarded the franchise are once again able to cream off a profit at the public's expense.

It has been calculated that the privatisation of the railways had already cost a minimum of £11 billion by 2010,[15] once dividend payments, fragmentation costs, the "sunk costs" involved in the privatisation (underselling the ROSCOs, and writing-off debts/ transferring liabilities in order to sell off Railtrack), and the costs of excessive interest payments on Network Rail's borrowing on the private market are taken into account. If this sum had gone into reducing fares, it would have resulted in an across-the-board reduction of fares of some 18%,[16] helping households significantly with the affordability of rail travel.

On the buses

Though less well publicised than the effects of rail privatisation, the deregulation of the bus market has been equally disastrous, particularly outside London. Although not a sexy issue for the media, buses really matter to millions of us. After all, people make more than 5 billion journeys by bus every year, more than three times the number of train journeys, and more than one in eight people in Britain rely on the bus in order to get to work.[17]

Bus services are a social good

For the young, buses are essential for getting to college or finding work, while for elderly people bus travel offers a vital link to overcome isolation. People who live in rural communities are particularly reliant on affordable and regular bus services, the lack of which falls particularly on the poorest, who are less able to afford car ownership or expensive taxi journeys. Getting more of us taking the bus would also be useful to relieve congestion on our roads, to help people find work, get to college or the shops (good for economic growth), and to reduce carbon emissions to tackle climate change. More and better bus services, affordable, convenient and accessible, would be a social good.

Sadly, thanks to a combination of deregulation to allow private profiteers to dominate bus services and the impact of austerity cuts to public spending, the trends are all going in the wrong direction. The title of the Campaign for Better Transport's report "Buses in Crisis" is no exaggeration. Figures from the RMT union suggest that since 1995 bus fare increases have outstripped inflation by over 40%. That's if your bus service hasn't been cut altogether. As CfBT report, since 2010 over £56 million has been cut from supported bus services, with many routes and services being cut completely. In the south east of England alone 160 bus services have been cut or withdrawn since 2011,[18] and a similar pattern is replicated across the country. As fares have rocketed overall passenger numbers have consistently fallen, with the number of bus journeys outside London down by 36% since deregulation in 1986.

Big five exploit monopolies

So what's been going so wrong? The Competition Commission has been forced to acknowledge both the failure of deregulation to provide effective competition, with 70% of services provided by just five operators: Arriva, FirstGroup, Go-Ahead, National Express and Stagecoach. Head-to-head competition between providers was said to be "uncommon" and "many local markets exhibit persistently high levels of concentration".[19] In other words, in many of our major towns and cities a single operator tends to dominate the market to the exclusion of competitors, and is able to use this advantage to force passengers to pay higher fares. Indeed, the investigation found evidence that, at least in the north east of England, bus operators were agreeing to carve up areas between themselves so that they could enjoy such local monopolies.

Before bus services were opened up to for-profit operators, publicly owned and operated bus companies could cross-subsidise services, so "profitable" routes could help to support routes which were socially necessary but not viable in purely commercial terms. With deregulation, private bus operators can cherry-pick which services to operate, concentrating on those which allow them to make money while withdrawing less profitable services unless local authorities stump up extra cash. The government doesn't even record centrally how many services are withdrawn by private operators, with no legal requirement on the latter to consult the communities affected.

As with the privatised railways, bus operators continue to extract huge subsidies from the taxes we pay and ever-increasing fare revenue from passengers. In 2012-13, all local UK bus services generated £5.5 billion revenue for operators – 76% of that was from passenger revenue, including the concessionary bus fare scheme subsidised by the public. While the concessionary fare scheme should continue, it was a source of £810m in revenue to private bus operators outside London in the last year alone. As such, under the current deregulated system, this significant subsidy is not reinvested in the industry and instead makes a major contribution to the profits of Stagecoach, Arriva, National Express, Go-Ahead and First Group.

The deregulated market's estimated annual value is around £4 billion and the big five transport companies make no secret of their plans to target it to increase their profits, in direct conflict with the interests of passengers, bus workers and the taxpayer. This blatant profiteering must be met with a strong regulatory response by government if this pattern is to be stopped and bus services returned to serving the interests of passengers, bus workers and society.

It should also be noted that bus workers, as well as passengers, have been hit hard by the deregulation in the bus industry. In 1985 bus workers were, rightly highly valued, and earned 7% above the average weekly wage in the UK – today they work four hours more but are paid 14% less a week than the average UK worker.

Local cuts see buses cut or withdrawn

Currently 78% of bus services outside of London are run by for-profit operators, while 22% are subsidised or supported by local authorities.[20] The latter include services to communities which would otherwise be totally cut off from the public transport network, evening or weekend services that commercial operators cannot run at a profit, or other socially necessary services. The ability of local authorities to maintain such support has been drastically undermined by the coalition government cuts to their budgets. As the Campaign for Better Transport explains:

> As part of the coalition government's Spending Review in 2010 it was announced that government funding to local authorities for transport would be cut by 28 per cent; and that the Bus Service Operators' Grant (BSOG) – which provides direct support for all bus services – would be cut by 20 per cent from 2012-13. In addition, the Department for Transport changed the formula for funding local authorities for the statutory free travel scheme for older people and those with disabilities. The effect of this formula change has been a cut of around £60m for local authorities. This under-funding of the concessionary fares scheme means that less funding is available for supported services. With such reductions it is unsurprising that councils are making cuts to services. Delivering the same level of bus services, and responding to increased demand for some services, while nearly 30 per cent of funding has been taken out of budgets represents a huge challenge for local authorities, a challenge that inevitably many find impossible to meet.[21]

Some councils have been able to protect supported bus services to a greater extent than others, but with the burden of the cuts falling most heavily on those council areas with greatest social need, the impact has been most severe in some of the least affluent areas of the country. Towns like Hartlepool and Darlington have eliminated all spending on supported bus services, while towns and cities across the south and east of England slashed their spending, in some cases by in excess of 40%.

Lack of public transport options punishes the vulnerable

Bus services are particularly important for those on low incomes with only 30% of the poorest households and 40% of households including disabled people[22] owning a car.[23] Although the cost of motoring has not risen as quickly as public transport, the combination of purchasing a vehicle, paying the road tax, insurance and getting it MOTed are all substantial hurdles for poor households, even before the cost of fuel is taken into account. Nevertheless, low paid and part-time workers are sometimes left with no choice but to put this additional major pressure on their family finances given the lack of available public transport options. The poorest fifth of the population take roughly three times the number of bus trips as the richest fifth, but with the cuts and withdrawals of service these same low-income households for whom car ownership is out of reach are now forced to take more taxi journeys than any other section of the population.[24]

At the same time the big five private operators continue to make huge profits from their tightening grip on the industry. According to consultants LEK, their profit margins have been running at 11.2%, prompting even then the transport minister Norman Baker to complain, "We have to ask ourselves why it is that the cost of bus travel has gone by up so much while bus company profitability is extremely healthy".[25]

Lower fares AND better services – only under public ownership

Yet the performance of the remaining municipally owned bus companies – operating in cities including Newport, Blackpool, Nottingham, Cardiff, Edinburgh and Reading – suggests that this model is capable of offering excellent passenger services and cheaper fares. But if the present crisis in bus provision is allowed to continue this will "undermine... policies to promote growth, reduce unemployment and tackle welfare dependency", while also affecting the poorest households most heavily, leading to the social isolation of elderly people and to greater pollution, congestion and carbon emissions.

The previous Labour government's introduction of Quality Contract Schemes for the regulation of local bus services offers some potential but is blighted by the excessive levels of bureaucracy required to introduce them. As a result, no local authority has a QCS, over a decade after they were introduced. The real key to regaining control over bus services is ownership of the fleet and clearer democratic accountability for local bus services, which is where municipally owned services have significant advantages.

The withdrawal of essential services is not a "price worth paying" in order to keep excessive fare increases under control. The idea that we must accept one or the other is utterly false. Take the example of London Underground. In total, fares on public transport in London have risen by 13.2% above inflation since 2009.[26] Some 84% of passengers report that fares are too high.[27] But Transport for London's "solution" to keeping costs down is to remove all ticket offices from London Underground stations, which is certainly not something that passengers are demanding. Indeed, the travelling public are rightly concerned about the potential implications for safety and levels of service.

The real inefficiencies lay elsewhere, with the disastrous Public-Private Partnership, the bloated salaries of senior managers, the complex interfaces between London Underground, track operating companies, engineering sub-contractors, outsourced cleaning firms and all the rest of the elaborate structure through which the network has been opened up to the interest of private profit. The answer is not to keep a lid on costs by undermining services and attacking the pay and conditions of the workforce, but to restructure the network to operate for the public good rather than for the dividends of shareholders.

The change we need

▸ Bring the railways back into public ownership, with passenger and worker representation in the operational management and strategic management of the network
▸ Use the savings from renationalisation to reduce fares and invest in infrastructure
▸ Promote the use of rail freight to alleviate congestion and pollution on the roads
▸ Allow local authorities to take local bus services back under municipal ownership, including the option of a municipally owned and operated bus fleet
▸ Create strategic transport authorities outside London with passenger and worker representation, with effective powers to regulate transport fares, requiring profit-making companies to cross-subsidise the provision of socially necessary services
▸ Keep ticket offices open on London Underground, and reunify the track, maintenance and operation of passenger services under public ownership
▸ Mandate the introduction of a flexible fares structure across public transport for part-time workers

▶ Defend funding of concessionary travel entitlements, including pensioners' bus passes
▶ Invest in creation of cycle lanes and development of green transport
▶ Increase charges on domestic flights.

9
Cost of Telecoms and Media

In two decades information technology and digital media made a massive forward leap. When the last Tory government left office in 1997 the mobile phone was only beginning to develop. Those were the days when yuppies on the stock exchange floor would hold something the size of a house brick. This was soon to become a basic device with widespread applications. In 1997/98, household ownership of mobile phones stood at 20 per cent of UK households, a figure that grew to 78 per cent over the next decade.[1]

At this time email was just emerging as a technology which was more convenient than fax machines. The internet was still in its infancy as a mass household facility; most were reliant on slow dial-up connections. The world of apps and high-speed digital downloads of content such as full-length films or albums were still a distant prospect. With neither wifi nor smartphones yet invented, both would be accessed only via personal computers tethered by leads. Laptop computers were relatively crude and heavy, and the advent of the iPad and the tablet almost unimaginable.

Tories help out Sky

Meanwhile television was still for the most part very much in analogue mode, with some viewers (though not all because of the signal strength) beginning to receive Channel 5 in additional to the other four regular network channel programmes.

Rupert Murdoch's Sky platform took advantage of the Tory government's generous arrangements to dominate the new field of satellite broadcasting, subsuming its main rival British Satellite Broadcasting (BSB) at the start of the 1990s.

Scandalously, although BBC programmes continue to be among the most popular with viewers on Sky's platform, the licence fee payer has been required to subsidise Murdoch's profits in the form of the retransmission fees that the BBC has to pay Sky for the privilege of having its content carried.

Meanwhile, the launch of the Ondigital service (which would ultimately face a financial crisis and go into administration) was only just around the corner. But its set-top boxes, and those of the cable TV pioneers, were initially only available as part of a "pay-TV" model, meaning that the explosion of choice offered in the digital world was still unfamiliar to most viewers.

Public sector innovates, private sector profits

The communications landscape has changed utterly since then and with it has come an increasing range of commodified services that viewers need to fork out to avoid "digital exclusion". Prior to this the key telecoms and media expansion most households were covered by the cost of a telephone landline and a TV licence – which, prior to the privatisation of British Telecom in 1984, were both paid to publicly owned companies that could reinvest revenues in improving services.

It is far from the case that privatisation delivered rapid progress. In fact the most significant innovations in the communications revolutions have their origin in research and development carried out in the public sector, then private profiteers were allowed to cash in on these breakthroughs. As economics professor Mariana Mazzucato observes in her important study *The Entrepreneurial State*, key advances like the creation of the internet, touchscreen technology and GPS location-tracking arose from research and development funded by the state in the context of defence and military priorities. But having paid once through our taxes to foster such innovations, we are now stung again since it has been left to profit-hungry private corporations to exploit the subsequent take-up.

BT's private monopoly

The new private shareholders of BT – who inherited what was in effect a monopoly position – were allowed to exploit their early head start. Of the 25 million residential landlines in the UK, BT still remains by far the largest provider, enjoying a market share 25% greater than its nearest competitor Virgin Media.[2] Is this because BT offers the best value for money? Hardly, back in 2008 a basic phone line rental with BT cost £11.50. In 2015 it cost £16.99 (over £200 a year, excluding call costs or broadband services), a percentage increase of around 47%. In the same year many phone and internet services were scheduled to increase by 6.49%, four times the rate of inflation.[3] The 1571 answerphone service, which used to be free, now costs £22.20 per year on top of the line rental.

For an increasing number of people, now that mobile phone contracts come on contracts with inclusive minutes, the landline is retained only for broadband access rather than for making calls. But BT's original near-monopoly on landline contracts has handed it a big advantage when it comes to fixed broadband provision, with more than 3 in 10 consumers remaining with BT for their internet access.[4] However, despite their competitive advantage, BT had been slow to roll out the infrastructure to extend super-fast broadband access to rural communities, since to do so might not be profitable. This has meant that over 5.3 million premises have lacked fast broadband access, leaving rural consumers and businesses alike still suffering with what used to be dubbed "world-wide wait".

Recognising the problem, the coalition government promised a £1.2 billion subsidy to remedy the situation. The influential public accounts select committee of MPs was highly critical of the way this was handled: out of 44 contracts with local bodies publicly subsidised to ensure that coverage was extended to rural areas, BT was ultimately awarded all 44. So much for competition! BT was allowed to abuse its position as the main provider of telecoms infrastructure, and the coverage maps of existing provision were not disclosed so rival bidders could compete.[5]

Digital exclusion

Rural communities are not alone in suffering from the effects of "digital exclusion". While the phenomenon of the "silver surfer" or digitally-savvy pensioners is now firmly established and growing all the time, ONS figures show that 5.7 million of the 10 million Britons over 65 have never used the internet.[6] In a survey for the internet provider Plusnet, 41% of those older people without internet access cited lack of understanding and inadequate training as the main reason.[7] However, ONS figures show that 13% of households of all ages without access cite the cost of hardware while 12% cite the cost of access.[8]

Unsurprisingly, poorer households are more likely to lack internet access at home – with the e-Learning Foundation highlighting last year that 750,000 school age children are unable to access the internet at home, and 650,000 lack access to a computer.[9] This means that young people from disadvantaged backgrounds are in danger of losing out both educationally and socially, a problem only compounded by the closures of public libraries, even if the advent of relatively affordable tablets and smartphones might help to close this digital gap, with around eight in ten 13-18 year olds now owning such devices.[10]

Wrong tariff rip-off

While not everyone has a smartphone, at least 92% of UK households now use some kind of mobile phone.[11] But are we getting value for money from the mobile providers? Ofcom figures do show that call and data charges have been falling at a time when the roll-out of 3G and 4G technology has improved services significantly. At the same time, however, UK consumers are reported to spend £5 billion too much for the mobile services they use, owing to being on the wrong tariff.[12]

Around seven million different deals are believed to exist across the spectrum of mobile operators in the UK. This further undermines the idea that more consumer choice is always a good thing. Very few people have the time or inclination to track down exactly which tariff provides the most accurate fit in meeting our specific patterns of call usage or data consumption, and to swap and change when either our behaviour or the terms of the contract change.

No signal misery

The needless fragmentation and profit-driven competition between private mobile phone networks also limits network coverage, since each of the operators has no incentive to share access to its signal masts. The result is that the frustration of having "no bars" and being unable to make or receive calls is experienced more than is technically necessary. Some customers found they couldn't be released from their contracts even though they could not receive a signal for much of the time.[13] As Dr Oliver Holland of King's College London's Centre for Telecommunications Research has argued:

> Each mobile phone company is allotted a slice of the frequency spectrum. But at any given time, lots of

customers belonging to one company may be using their mobile phones. "You will probably have a reduction in the quality of the service, because they're all competing for the spectrum." Customers belonging to another company may be using the service less at the same time, leaving their slice of the spectrum to go to waste when others need it. "If you had just one body, instead of dividing the spectrum into chunks, they can use it more efficiently," he says.[14]

As Owen Jones has argued recently:

> The case for nationalising mobile phone companies is actually pretty overwhelming. It would mean an integrated network, with masts serving customers on the basis of need, rather than subordinating the needs of users to the needs of shareholders. Profits could be reinvested in research and development, as well as developing effective customer services. Rip-off practices could be eradicated.[15]

Costly calls

And there are plenty such practices to eliminate. Citizens Advice received over 28,000 complaints about mobile phone companies last year alone. One major problem is that our mobile bills are often higher than the nominal monthly rate of our contracts, either because we exceed our allowances, or make calls to numbers beginning 0870, 0844 or 0845 which are not deemed inclusive calls. These numbers – widely used by businesses and also by public sector bodies – can cost up to 40p per minute. 63% of calls made to all government departments used such numbers, including calls to Jobcentre Plus, the Department of Work and

Pensions, and HMRC. Even people in debt phoning Citizens Advice itself have been charged at these high rates. Worse still, directory enquiries numbers beginning 118 are premium rate services and can cost as much as £3 per minute on mobiles.

But the phenomenon of "bill shock" is not confined to excessive call charges. One of the most common reasons for unexpectedly high bills is the extra charges levied by phone companies for use in other countries (especially outside the EU) in cases where an agreement has not been made in advance with a UK provider. Call charges can be up to £1.50 per minute, whilst the cost of accessing the internet via "data roaming" abroad can mount up into hundreds or even thousands of pounds, leaving people with a nasty shock when they get home.

Commodifying play

The trend to commodify aspects of mobile phone games via "in-app purchases" has also meant that parents are increasingly in danger of finding their children have run up vast bills from playing simple games on their phones and tablets, paying to "buy" extra lives, make different moves, get better tools or reach different levels of the game. One dad reported that his two children, 6 and 8, had together run up a bill of £3,200 buying virtual food for their farm animals, spending "cash" that had a value that was all too real.[16]

New platforms

Notwithstanding the legitimate concern of workers in the creative industries that their rights over their own work are being undermined, such is the ease with which images, music and e-books can be illegally reproduced or shared, it is also the case that there has been an explosion in platforms for paid-for content to be legally accessed. Today's consumer can pay to download millions of songs from iTunes or to stream them via a service like Spotify, and purchase and immediately access a vast array of books published anywhere in the world – although were it not for the inevitable resistance of the profiteers, a publicly-owned platform for digital content could allow us to "borrow" access to such a vast array of materials for free on a temporary basis, similar to the public lending library but on a colossal scale.

The world of TV on-demand – BBC iPlayer and similar services – means that we are witnessing an increasingly rapid convergence between media, so that television is no longer just a box in the corner of the living room (or flatscreen on the wall for that matter), but something consumed on the go, on tablets or phones. BT, for example, is moving from providing broadband access to providing subscription TV and online content with its new BT Sport channel.

Similarly, traditional "linear" TV channels are facing increasing competition from the streaming on-demand services, including paid content like big Hollywood movies and premium US television programmes via services like Netflix. If the DVD box set began to accustom viewers to paying to watch favourite TV series then the likes of Netflix goes one stage further and begins to normalise the idea of paying to discover new programmes, shopping around for the latest "must-see". The danger of this model is the erosion of public and even commercially operated "free-to-air" broadcasting (such as ITV) in favour of premium content being put behind a paywall.

BBC – value for money

There are already calls by those trying to undermine the public service broadcasting ethos of the BBC that we should scrap the TV licence fee and force the BBC to compete on the lines of commercial subscription operators. The BBC has certainly had its fair share of problems of late but – despite the cuts that have resulted from a poorly negotiated licence fee settlement, the internal culture of bullying and abuse and its remote, over-paid and top-heavy managerial regime, all of which must be urgently addressed – the public still greatly values BBC programming and has no appetite for it to be destroyed. In fact, at around 40p a day the BBC is one of the few areas of national life where we do not feel ripped off – it's a bargain.

At the same time that it has cost us less in real terms, the fee now pays for so much more than the two high-quality entertainment channels, a network of local radio stations and four national radio stations – we now have BBC3 (regrettably scheduled to become digital-only) and BBC4, BBC News Channel, one of the country's most popular websites, TV and radio on demand via the BBC iPlayer, digital radio channels such as BBC 6 Music and the Asian Network, news, sport and weather apps and the World Service;[17] and all largely without commercial advertising. It is pretty hard to feel ripped off when we get all that for less than the cost of a pint of milk.

In the public interest

One of the major pluses that a national public service broadcaster like the BBC offers is to enable a common series of cultural reference points, with millions of viewers tuning in simultaneously, uniting a diverse range of households into a common viewing community. As BBC director general Tony Hall can rightly boast, "Just one in 25 Americans watched the biggest episode of Breaking Bad on a US subscription channel, compared to one in five of us Brits watching Sherlock on BBC1".[18]

Similarly, millions enjoyed British successes at the London Olympics on the Beeb, whilst England's latest Test Cricket series win could only be glimpsed later on terrestrial TV on Channel 5's highlights programme or via an expensive satellite subscription. To receive all Sky's channels would currently cost £948 a year (excluding the cost of installation and Sky Box Office or Sky Store content) and even then to watch all the Premiership football matches you'd need to pay a further £162, taking the total to well into four figures.

For the fanatical sports fan this might still feel worth it. But to abandon the TV licence to turn the BBC into a corporate profiteer running a subscription service in competition with the likes of Sky would be to jeopardise its world-renowned reputation for quality independent public service broadcasting in favour of the more commercially lucrative lowest common denominator. This would also inevitably widen cultural inequalities, and turn the experience of the best television into an exclusive privilege enjoyed by those in a position to afford multiple subscriptions to pay-TV providers.

The change we need

▸ Defend and reform the BBC as a world-class public service broadcaster, and ensure an above-inflation settlement for the TV licence under the terms of its next Charter renewal – but limit the salaries and pay-offs of senior management so that money is invested in frontline journalism and programming, not executive pay and bureaucracy

▸ Make commercial subscription services pay re-transmission fees to the BBC for re-broadcasting licence fee funded content

▸ Ring-fence live broadcasting rights for more high-profile sporting events to free-to-air terrestrial providers

▸ Ensure that profitable internet-based services or retailers such as Google and Amazon pay their fair share of taxes to the UK exchequer

▶ Require broadband providers to offer free public wifi access points in all council housing or social housing developments

▶ Launch a publicly owned "virtual library" platform to allow UK citizens temporary legal access to a wide variety of films, music and e-books as a digital equivalent to the public library

▶ Provide schools with a bank of laptops and tablets to loan to poorer children whose education might be suffering from lack of internet access

▶ Prevent mobile phone operators from restricting spectrum usage for their competitors, not only for phone calls but for data, and automatically switch customers to the lowest available tariff matching their monthly usage

▶ Cap the cost of 0845, 0870 and 0844 numbers when accessed from a mobile to the same level as a landline, and ensure that all advice lines of public bodies use freephone numbers.

10

Conclusion

There can be little doubt that the talk of a "cost of living crisis" reflects the reality for millions of households across the UK. We have seen the real value of wages suffer the most sustained squeeze on records, benefits slashed, and a new "flexible" model of low paid, part-time jobs taking in-work poverty to record levels, the outlook for the incomes of ordinary families remains bleak. Add into the mix the unaffordability of home ownership for millions, sky-high private rents, the precarious ability of many to repay the mortgage if interest rates go up and the erosion of secure tenure in the social rented sector and the picture of misery is worse still. And that's before the soaring cost of everyday essentials, with food up 46% and electricity 73% since 2005.[1]

This has not happened accidentally but, rather, is the result of a sustained ideologically-driven assault aimed at decimating public spending in order to create new markets for private companies to profit from selling services previously provided by the state. It has been part of a deliberate strategy to transfer resources from services which benefit the majority, and which are particularly vital for the most vulnerable sections of society, in order that a very few at the top can extend their already obscene wealth at our expense. As US billionaire investor Warren Buffet candidly admitted, "There's class warfare, all right, but it's my class, the rich class, that's making war, and we're winning".[2]

But whilst politicians in Westminster have traded blows about the pace and scale of the cuts, all the main parties have been united in urging the need for "fiscal prudence", and emphasising the over-riding need to "balance the books". This, despite the fact that failing to put money in the pockets of the lowest income earners – those most likely to spend it, and hence grow the economy – has actually ensured that the Coalition's plan to eliminate the deficit over five years would go wildly awry. Yet the reality is that the decision to pursue austerity has been a choice, to unleash a vicious and entirely avoidable assault on what economists call the "social wage" rather than make big corporate and financial interests pay for the crisis they created.

George Osborne, in his Autumn Statement of 2014, revealed that the bulk of the planned cuts are yet to come with a further 60% to follow in the next five years to 2020. In a chilling warning, the "independent" Office of Budget Responsibility admitted that this would take public spending in Britain to a level not seen since the 1930s.[3] But whilst Labour rightly warns that such plans would be impossible to implement without a catastrophic impact on frontline services, the fact remains that Labour's own spending plans – based on a commitment to return to a budget surplus in the next parliament – will also entail cuts to services or higher taxes. The commitment to continue the pay freeze across the public sector will effectively mean a real-terms cut in the incomes of a raft of key workers like teachers, nurses, and dinnerladies.

Since basics such as heating and public transport are rising faster than other items and take up a greater percentage of what low-income households spend than is the case for the wealthy, even if wages and benefits kept pace with CPI inflation, the effect would still be a cut in the real value of the incomes for low earners. A government genuinely interested in helping families with the cost of living crisis would need at the very least to protect the real value of pay, by pegging increases to a measure which reflects the differences in the effective rate of inflation paid across the distribution scale, like NEF's Real Britain Index (RBI).[4]

There is a glaring contradiction between an opposition which offers, on the one hand, to help families with the rising cost of living they accurately diagnose, yet at the same time remains committed to continue wielding the axe on public services, whilst further squeezing wages and raising taxes. There is a clear trade-off involved between the ability to prioritise action on the cost of living and meeting promises to continue with austerity (albeit at a slower pace than the Tories).

Quality of life under attack

While this analysis concentrates on the cost of living in primarily financial terms, it is of course impossible to isolate monetary costs from all those other costs to our quality of life – working ever longer hours so you do not have time to enjoy free time and relax; feeling more anxious, uncertain or depressed about our lives; experiencing services where targets and profits come before the dignity of the human beings; living in an environment which is damaged so that a rich elite can prosper. None of these things are necessarily disclosed by raw figures like GDP that measure economic output.

For all the talk about the economy's return to recovery, the "feelgood factor" is absent. With an economy where rewards are so skewed to the top 1%, people simply do not feel that the proceeds of growth will be felt equally. The "recovery" – itself built on the unsustainable basis of a house price bubble – does not ring true for millions of working people. When it comes to austerity, we are told "we're all this together", but when it comes to the recovery many of us feel left out completely. Cameron and Clegg gloat about having created more new jobs in the economy, but in reality these are low paid, low-skilled jobs on zero hours contracts, or bogus self-employment. It's increasingly common for people to have to work two, three or more such jobs to keep their heads above water.

Unions needed more than ever

While this picture has got significantly worse following the financial crisis of 2008 and the austerity regime that followed in its wake, these problems have their basis in structural changes that successive governments have sought to deliver since the mid-late 1970s – the familiar litany of neoliberal measures which Thatcher did so much to introduce, and New Labour pretended could be squared with social justice.

It is no coincidence that this period was inaugurated with an outright attack on trade unions via a series of measures that put legal and administrative hurdles in the way of their ability to take strike action, conduct solidarity (secondary) picketing, maintain closed-shop agreements and more. So, too, the spate of privatisation and outsourcing has been part and parcel of a deliberate attack on the collective bargaining power of trade unions.

It is clear from David Cameron's rhetoric on introducing thresholds for strike ballots that his zeal to further contain trade union influence is far from diminished. The fact that the average tube driver on London Underground earns over £50,000 is surely sufficient evidence of how a well organised union like the RMT with a fighting leadership prepared to stand up to management is capable of defending pay and conditions to an extent that poorly organised sectors can only envy.

Far from being outdated "dinosaurs", trade unions are more necessary than ever in reversing the damage of the last few decades and helping ordinary people fight for a better future. We saw just what a difference having strong trade unions, and a framework of collective bargaining meant for Burger King workers in Denmark in comparison to their counterparts working for the same chain in the US. But the social importance of trade unions lies not only in securing better pay and conditions for their members (though this is vital), but also in their ability to defend the interests of working people from the effects of the cuts and privatisation of vital public services used not only by trade unionists and their families but also the wider community.

Costs beyond prices

Tackling rising prices, taken in isolation, is not enough. Take, for instance, the price of food. With food banks on the rise it might be thought a good thing that discounter supermarkets like Aldi and Lidl are prompting a price war and forcing the market leaders to compete. Needless to say, however, corporate bosses and shareholders are not willing to take a hefty hit in terms of lower bonuses and reduced dividends. Instead, to protect their profit margins, the screw is turned on their suppliers, who are pushed to deliver the product to the retailer at the lowest possible cost.

Unless there is some unexpected increase in productivity (e.g. through more efficient machinery) or decrease in the cost of raw materials, then the cost saving can only be delivered by either lowering the quality of the inputs or by undermining the pay and conditions of employees. The result is a combination of deteriorating animal welfare under intensive production techniques, pressure to adulterate ingredients (remember the scandal around horse-meat in ready meals?), and greater exploitation for the workforce. Keeping a lid on prices is not an end in itself, especially if it means that the incomes of millions of working households are hit as a consequence. Being able to buy a cheaper pie is not such a good thing if you don't trust what's inside of it, or you're the one getting paid less to make it.

It should also be remembered that the increased burden austerity has imposed is not felt in purely financial terms. When Cameron points to the overall rise in the number of jobs in the economy, he neglects to say how many are part-time and low-paid, with people increasingly forced to take hold down two or even more jobs. More of us are working unpaid overtime too. According to TUC figures:

> over 5.4 million workers are putting in around £640 million worth of unpaid hours every week... [the number] regularly doing unpaid hours at work increased by 331,000 last year to 5.42m – the biggest annual rise since comparable records began in 1998. The proportion of people doing unpaid overtime is at its highest-ever level (21.2 per cent of the UK workforce), while the average amount of unpaid overtime has also reached a record high of 7 hours 48 minutes a week.

Even when we leave the workplace, we're having to put in extra unpaid shifts looking after children, or disabled, sick or elderly family or friends. Thus we find ourselves paying for cuts to public services with our available free time. Even where care services are in place, with 60% of councils now introducing 15 minute short care visits[5] the often poorly paid care workers face increased stress and time pressure whilst the care user experiences a level of service that feels cursory and inadequate. Where local facilities like libraries or leisure centres are cut, whole communities lose out, not necessarily in financial terms but in terms of their learning, health and overall quality of life.

Structural change is needed

Genuinely addressing the cost of living crisis requires more than superficial gestures. Take Labour's pre-election pledge to freeze energy prices for two years. While it is not unwelcome, how are we to be sure that the companies won't offset the cost by hiking up prices in advance, or cut back on levels of investment or staff pay rather than take a hit to their profits? A new regulator would still face intense pressure from the well-resourced lobbying operations of a privately owned energy industry, and would not resolve the basic issue that utilities that should be run for the public good are instead being run according to the demands of private profiteers. Similarly, although we want cheaper train fares, we do not want this to be at the expense of cuts that undermine safety.

What would it mean to genuinely make reversing the cost of living crisis a key priority in government? The action required is not compatible with continuing with an agenda which seeks to limit the public sector in order to create new markets for private profit, the very forces responsible for the economic crash in the first place. Rather, we need fundamental structural changes to put people rather than profit at the heart of the economy. We should be looking to bringing the production and distribution of goods and services back under public ownership and democratic accountability.

Does this mean turning the clock back to monolithic state-owned bureaucracies? By no means. But too often when politicians talk about decentralising power they are effectively trying to divest responsibilities from the state, without providing the resources and structures necessary for local communities to genuinely determine how services are run. Power, here, is not devolved but relinquished, with the market only too ready to step into the void, meaning that "choice" is available only for those who can afford it. But authentic decentralisation of power could bring workers, service-users and local communities together to collectively make decisions over the distribution of resources.

It could be objected that the radical action we have outlined is simply too costly to deliver. Yet far from imposing a burden on public funds, much of what is proposed here would liberate significant resources from their current use in subsidising the profits of the rich. There would be no direct cost to the state in ensuring that workers have sufficient legal protections to guarantee collective bargaining power. Strengthening trade union rights would make sure that workers can protect their incomes from being squeezed by the unchecked power of profit-hungry corporations. Instead of money subsidising profitable employers paying poverty wages, it should protect the benefit incomes of those in need. The housing benefit bill is subsidising fat cat landlords profiting from sky-high rents, when rent controls could keep housing affordable and save money too.

Ultimately running services for the public good rather than private profit will also be a more efficient way of spending resources. Why do we waste money subsiding an industry like rail so that shareholders of private corporations can walk off with millions while the travelling public pays more to use overcrowded and unreliable train services? Why do we let so much money get wasted on legal fees, accountants' fees, and all the rest of the army of bureaucrats needed to prepare endless rounds of franchise bids?

Even a Tory-led government has had to recognise that it is cheaper for a not-for-profit body like Network Rail to be financed through the public sector than via the private market. Far from slashing public spending to make more room for private companies to make a killing, it's surely time to take back the production of key goods and services into public ownership. On the railways this could be done at next to no cost, by simply taking each expiring franchise back into public ownership and reunifying the whole system when the final private franchise has expired.

Radically different choices

No doubt critics will say the spending implications are "unrealistic". Firstly, some of the proposals – to crack down on in-work poverty by insisting that employers pay a decent living wage, or introduce effective rent controls – would save money from the welfare budget. Currently welfare spending is effectively used to bail out bosses who make millions by paying poverty wages and subsidise landlords through housing benefit. But extra resources could also be found via a radical shift in other spending priorities, such as saving billions on the planned replacement of the Trident nuclear defence system and ending the vast subsidy that goes to owners of private train operating companies.

And what about all the millions owed by multinational corporations like Starbucks, Google and Amazon who manage to order their tax affairs in order to avoid paying their fare share from the profits they make in this country? The City of London is the nexus of a whole series of Crown dependencies which are run as tax-havens: the Cayman Islands, British Virgin Islands, Jersey and Isle of Man. Up to £32 trillion is believed to be secretly squirreled in such offshore jurisdictions, deliberately out of reach of the public exchequer. Tax expert Richard Murphy estimates that the current "tax gap" from tax avoidance, evasion and late payments to be running at a colossal £119.4 billion,[6] enough to eliminate the budget deficit at a stroke.

Yet rather than crack down on this corporate greed, and stop obscenely wealthy oligarchs from living in Britain as "nom-doms" (non-domiciled for tax purposes), successive governments have slashed staffing at Her Majesty's Revenue and Customs (HMRC), which has seen jobs cut by more than half since 2005. This is a classic "false economy" since these cuts only further impair the ability to recover tax liabilities for the public purse. So why should we apologise for demanding that more money should end up going into the pockets of ordinary working people rather than being stashed in offshore tax havens or going to bail out banks that brought the economy to the edge of collapse? Ultimately it is a question of priorities.

Whenever it's a war or a weather emergency in the Tory shires, "money", as David Cameron once put it, "is no object". When the banks were judged "too big to fail" we spent billions bailing them out from the consequences of their own greed. So why is it that governments are prepared to fail millions of people across Britain, making us work harder and longer, in jobs that pay less, and have less of a safety net if we lose our jobs, fall ill or become disabled? Why are we paying through the nose for essential goods and services so the mega-rich at the top can make their billions? Never again should we allow a tiny elite at the top to impose policies that are so blatantly in the interests of a wealthy privileged class, at the expense of the majority.

It's not enough just to talk about the cost of living. The information in this book should leave no one in doubt that the austerity programme has failed. Worse, there are sinister undertones that threaten the concept of a caring society. The austerity project must be terminated immediately and all progressive movements mobilised to ensure its demise.

A government that genuinely made addressing the crisis a priority would scrap the pay freeze in the public sector, encourage wage-led recovery and protect the real value of welfare benefit payments. It would abandon Tory spending limits and invest in jobs and growth. And it would commit to bringing privatised and outsourced services back under public ownership and democratic management. In doing so, it would need to deliver on a promise first made by Labour over 40 years ago: to "bring about a fundamental and irreversible shift in the balance of power and wealth in favour of working people and their families". The reign of economic injustice which blights the lives of so many in Britain today must be brought to an end.

Endnotes

Chapter 1

1 http://www.ons.gov.uk/ons/rel/gva/gross-domestic-product--preliminary-estimate/q1-2014/stb-gdp-preliminary-estimate--q1-2014.html

2 http://www.ons.gov.uk/ons/rel/gva/gross-domestic-product--preliminary-estimate/q1-2014/stb-gdp-preliminary-estimate--q1-2014.html

3 ONS figures, cited http://www.bbc.co.uk/news/10604117

4 http://www.theguardian.com/uk-news/2014/may/15/britains-richest-1-percent-own-same-as-bottom-55-population

5 Howard Reed, http://blogs.lse.ac.uk/politicsandpolicy/archives/35827

6 http://www.independent.co.uk/travel/news-and-advice/rail-fare-increases-commuters-take-a-hit-as-ticket-prices-rise-three-times-faster-than-wages-9033028.html

7 http://www.ucu.org.uk/index.cfm?articleid=5211

8 http://www.parliament.uk/briefing-papers/sn05823.pdf

9 http://www.independent.co.uk/news/uk/politics/disaster-as-uk-housebuilding-rate-falls-away-8955242.html

10 https://england.shelter.org.uk/news/january_2013/housing_costs_cause_stress_and_depression_for_millions

11 http://www.housing.org.uk/publications/browse/home-truths-2013-14

12 http://www.resolutionfoundation.org/publications/closer-edge-prospects-household-debt-repayments-in/

13 http://www.realbritainindex.org/report/the-real-britain-index

14 http://budgetresponsibility.org.uk/economic-fiscal-outlook-december-2014/

15 http://yougov.co.uk/news/2013/11/04/nationalise-energy-and-rail-companies-say-public/

16 http://actionforrail.org/rmt-press-release-18-july-polling-for-rmt-throws-down-challenge-to-labour/

Chapter 2

1 http://highpaycentre.org/blog/fatcat-wednesday-for-ftse-100-ceos

2 http://www.theguardian.com/business/2014/jul/21/tesco-ousts-philip-clarke-after-profit-warning

3 http://www.payscale.com/research/UK/Job=Checkout_Operator/Hourly_Rate

4 http://www.livingwage.org.uk/what-living-wage

5 http://www.archbishopofyork.org/york//data/files/resources/3041/Living-Wage-Commission-Report-v2_f-1.pdf, p26

6 see Holmes, C and Mayhew, K, Are UK labour markets polarising? (University of Oxford, 2010), and http://www.resolutionfoundation.org/media/media/downloads/A_polarising_crisis.pdf

7 http://www.resolutionfoundation.org/media/media/downloads/Low_Pay_Britain_2013.pdf, p3

8 http://www.archbishopofyork.org/york//data/files/resources/3041/Living-Wage-Commission-Report-v2_f-1.pdf, p13

9 http://www.archbishopofyork.org/york//data/files/resources/3041/Living-Wage-Commission-Report-v2_f-1.pdf, p13

10 http://www.ons.gov.uk/ons/rel/elmr/an-examination-of-falling-real-wages/2010-to-2013/art-an-examination-of-falling-real-wages.html#tab-abstract

11 http://www.ifs.org.uk/comms/r81.pdf

12 http://www.ons.gov.uk/ons/rel/elmr/an-examination-of-falling-real-wages/2010-to-2013/art-an-examination-of-falling-real-wages.html#tab-Long-run-trends-in-real-wage-growth-

13 http://www.ons.gov.uk/ons/rel/regional-trends/regional-economic-analysis/changes-in-real-earnings-in-the-uk-and-london--2002-to-2012/sum-real-wages-down-by-8-5--since-2009.html

14 http://www.resolutionfoundation.org/media/media/downloads/The-State-of-Living-Standards-ResolutionFoundation-Audit2014.pdf

15 PwC UK Economic Outlook, cited, http://www.theguardian.com/society/2014/mar/11/public-sector-workers-earnings-squeeze

16 http://www.archbishopofyork.org/york//data/files/resources/3041/Living-Wage-Commission-Report-v2_f-1.pdf, p24

17 http://www.bbc.co.uk/news/business-26265858

18 http://siteframework.rss-hosting.co.uk/Shared_ASP_Files/UploadedFiles/rmt/823AE542-6D6F-4A7A-8986-1711B41E4AE9_contractorscharter-amended.pdf

19 http://ucatt.infobo.co.uk/files/publications/UCATT%20Report%20The%20Great%20Payroll%20Scandal%202012.pdf

20 http://www.parliament.uk/briefing-papers/sn06553.pdf

21 http://www.publicfinance.co.uk/news/2013/08/public-and-third-sector-biggest-users-of-zero-hours-contracts/

22 http://www.standard.co.uk/business/business-news/mps-call-for-zero-hours-contracts-to-be-abolished- 9258409.html

23 http://www.dartmouth.edu/~blnchflr/papers/Bell%20and%20Blanchflower.pdf

24 http://niesr.ac.uk/press/underemployment-uk-11285#.U05-VKJ7S-U

25 https://www.gov.uk/employment-rights-for-interns

26 http://www.publications.parliament.uk/pa/cm201314/cmhansrd/cm130618/halltext/130618h0001.htm

27 http://www.boycottworkfare.org/?page_id=663

28 http://www.boycottworkfare.org/?page_id=663

29 https://www.gov.uk/government/uploads/system/uploads/attachment_data/file/288847/The_National_Minimum_Wage_LPC_Report_2014.pdf, p134

30 https://www.gov.uk/government/uploads/system/uploads/
    attachment_data/file/288847/The_National_Minimum_Wage_LPC_
    Report_2014.pdf, p122

31 https://www.gov.uk/government/uploads/system/uploads/
    attachment_data/file/288847/The_National_Minimum_Wage_LPC_
    Report_2014.pdf, p133

32 http://www.publications.parliament.uk/pa/cm201314/cmhansrd/
    cm140306/debtext/140306-0001.htm#140306-0001.htm_wqn3

33 https://www.gov.uk/government/uploads/system/uploads/
    attachment_data/file/288847/The_National_Minimum_Wage_LPC_
    Report_2014.pdf, p31

34 https://www.gov.uk/government/uploads/system/uploads/
    attachment_data/file/288847/The_National_Minimum_Wage_LPC_
    Report_2014.pdf, p32

35 http://www.resolutionfoundation.org/media/media/downloads/Low_
    Pay_Britain_2013.pdf, p12

36 http://www.publications.parliament.uk/pa/ld201314/ldselect/
    ldeucom/164/16402.htm

37 http://www.resolutionfoundation.org/media/media/downloads/
    Starting_out_or_getting_stuck_FINAL_1.pdf

38 http://www.resolutionfoundation.org/media/media/downloads/Low_
    Pay_Britain_2013.pdf

39 http://www.ons.gov.uk/ons/rel/lmac/public-and-private-sector-
    earnings/march-2014/rpt---march-2014.html

40 https://www.gov.uk/government/news/public-sector-pay-awards-for-
    2014-15

41 Does performance-based pay improve teaching? PISA in Focus (May
    2012 issue), OECD

42 http://www.tuc.org.uk/equality-issues/gender-equality/equal-pay/
    shock-rise-gender-pay-gap-after-years-slow-steady-progress

43 see http://www.resolutionfoundation.org/media/media/downloads/ Low_Pay_Britain_2013.pdf, https://www.gov.uk/government/ publications/national-minimum-wage-low-pay-commission- report-2014, http://livingwagecommission.org.uk/wp-content/ uploads/2014/02/Living-Wage-Commission-Report-v2_f-1.pdf

44 http://www.nytimes.com/2014/10/28/business/international/living- wages-served-in-denmark-fast-food-restaurants.html?_r=0

45 http://www.theguardian.com/business/economics-blog/2014/apr/15/ earnings-above-inflation-dont-spend-all-at-once

Chapter 3

1 http://www.theguardian.com/lifeandstyle/2013/feb/20/1701-people- apply-for-eight-barista-jobs

2 https://www.gov.uk/government/uploads/system/uploads/attachment_ data/file/298468/outturn-and-forecast-budget-2014-summary-tables. xls

3 https://www.gov.uk/government/uploads/system/uploads/attachment_ data/file/298468/outturn-and-forecast-budget-2014-summary-tables. xls

4 http://www.centreforsocialjustice.org.uk/publications/signed-on- written-off

5 http://livingwagecommission.org.uk/wp-content/uploads/2014/02/ Living-Wage-Commission-Report-v2_f-1.pdf

6 http://www.leftfootforward.org/2012/06/uk-benefits-not-most- generous-in-europe/

7 http://www.pcs.org.uk/en/news_and_events/pcs_comment/index. cfm/id/C2889BD8-D6BA-4799-82FBA4DF9E986CB0

8 http://www.pcs.org.uk/en/news_and_events/pcs_comment/index. cfm/id/C2889BD8-D6BA-4799-82FBA4DF9E986CB0

9 http://www.theguardian.com/commentisfree/2011/nov/04/george- osborne-benefits-cheat

10 http://www.mirror.co.uk/night-copy/20billion-of-benefits-go- unclaimed-each-663004

11 http://www.bbc.co.uk/news/uk-26924411

12 http://www.bbc.co.uk/news/uk-26924411

13 http://www.dailymail.co.uk/news/article-2552850/Delays-Universal-Credit-mean-far-cost-225-000-EACH-person-new-benefits-system.html

14 http://www.theguardian.com/commentisfree/2013/jul/12/universal-credit-less-pay

15 http://www.theguardian.com/society/2014/feb/19/record-number-sanctions-benefits-claimants

16 http://www.theguardian.com/society/2014/feb/19/record-number-sanctions-benefits-claimants

17 http://welfaretales.wordpress.com/category/sanctions-2/

18 http://labourlist.org/2013/03/second-leaked-dwp-whistleblower-document-shows-welfare-sanctions-targets-are-widespread/

19 http://www.crisis.org.uk/data/files/publications/Crisis%20response%20to%20the%20Independent%20review%20of%20JSA%20sanctions%20call%20for%20information.pdf

20 http://www.dailymail.co.uk/news/article-2347281/Unemployed-graduate-benefits-stopped-missing-job-centre-appointment-INTERVIEW.html

21 https://twitter.com/PovertyAlliance/statuses/316531225198211072

22 http://stupidsanctions.tumblr.com/

23 http://www.welfareconditionality.ac.uk/wp-content/uploads/2013/12/sanctions-stats-briefing-d-webster-19-feb-2014.pdf

24 Citizens Advice, Punishing Poverty? http://sdrv.ms/1c48ECq

25 http://www.independent.co.uk/news/uk/politics/churches-unite-to-act-on-food-poverty-600-leaders-from-all-denominations-demand-government-uturn-on-punitive-benefits-sanctions-9263035.html

26 http://www.mirror.co.uk/news/uk-news/council-tax-huge-queues-outside-2033516

27 http://disabilityrightsuk.org/news/2013/june/risk-major-disability-poverty-rise

28 http://www.redpepper.org.uk/getting-rich-on-disability-denial/

29   http://www.mirror.co.uk/news/uk-news/benefits-assessments-atos-quits-government-3293634

30   http://www.theguardian.com/society/2012/may/23/gps-work-capability-assessment-scrapped

31   Phillips G. Time to put right what is going wrong in the government's disability assessments. BMJ 2013;347:f6014

32   http://www.publications.parliament.uk/pa/cm201213/cmselect/cmpubacc/744/74403.htm

33   http://www.citizensadvice.org.uk/index/pressoffice/press_index/press_20140125.htm

34   http://www.publications.parliament.uk/pa/cm201314/cmhansrd/cm140227/debtext/140227-0002.htm

35   http://www.publications.parliament.uk/pa/cm201314/cmhansrd/cm140227/debtext/140227-0002.htm

36   http://www.publications.parliament.uk/pa/cm201314/cmhansrd/cm140227/debtext/140227-0003.htm

37   http://www.publications.parliament.uk/pa/cm201314/cmhansrd/cm140227/debtext/140227-0002.htm

38   http://www.demos.co.uk/publications/copingwiththecuts

39   http://www.nao.org.uk/wp-content/uploads/2014/02/Personal-independence-payment-early- progress.pdf

40   http://www.pcs.org.uk/en/news_and_events/pcs_comment/index.cfm/relentless-welfare-attacks-highlighted-in-parliament

41   http://wowpetition.com/calums-list/

Chapter 4

1   http://www.independent.co.uk/news/uk/politics/disaster-as-uk-housebuilding-rate-falls-away-8955242.html

2   https://www.gov.uk/government/uploads/system/uploads/attachment_data/file/284648/English_Housing_Survey_Headline_Report_2012-13.pdf

3   http://www.housing.org.uk/publications/browse/home-truths-2013-14

4   https://england.shelter.org.uk/news/january_2013/1.4_million_
    britons_falling_behind_with_the_rent_or_mortgage

5   https://england.shelter.org.uk/news/january_2013/housing_costs_
    cause_stress_and_depression_for_millions

6   http://www.pricedout.org.uk/

7   http://england.shelter.org.uk/__data/assets/pdf_file/0004/721255/
    At_any_cost_final_int_FINAL.pdf

8   http://england.shelter.org.uk/professional_resources/policy_and_
    research/policy_library/policy_library_folder/food_for_thought

9   http://england.shelter.org.uk/__data/assets/pdf_file/0004/721255/
    At_any_cost_final_int_FINAL.pdf

10 https://www.gov.uk/government/uploads/system/uploads/attachment_
    data/file/284648/English_Housing_Survey_Headline_Report_2012-
    13.pdf

11 http://www.propertywire.com/news/europe/uk-buyers-deposits-rates-
    201403318951.html

12 http://www.theguardian.com/money/2013/dec/28/mortgage-rise-
    homeowners-perilous-debt

13 http://www.resolutionfoundation.org/publications/closer-edge-
    prospects-household-debt-repayments-in/

14 http://www.theguardian.com/money/2013/dec/28/mortgage-rise-
    homeowners-perilous-debt

15 http://www.telegraph.co.uk/finance/personalfinance/borrowing/
    mortgages/10392803/Aspiring-first-time-buyers-giving-up-hope-of-
    home-ownership-and-spending-instead.html

16 http://www.propertywire.com/news/europe/uk-buyers-deposits-rates-
    201403318951.html

17 http://england.shelter.org.uk/__data/assets/pdf_file/0003/681141/
    Shelter_-_A_Home_Of_Their_Own_Report.pdf

18 http://england.shelter.org.uk/__data/assets/pdf_file/0004/721255/
    At_any_cost_final_int_FINAL.pdf

19 Priced Out index report (February 2014), www.pricedout.org.uk

20 http://england.shelter.org.uk/__data/assets/pdf_file/0004/721255/
    At_any_cost_final_int_FINAL.pdf

21 http://england.shelter.org.uk/professional_resources/policy_and_
    research/policy_library/policy_library_folder/briefing_at_any_cost

22 http://www.theguardian.com/society/2014/feb/12/bedroom-tax-
    households-eviction-rent-arrears

23 http://my.knightfrank.com/research-reports/private-rented-sector-
    report.aspx

24 http://england.shelter.org.uk/__data/assets/pdf_file/0007/624391/
    Rent_trap_v4.pdf

25 http://england.shelter.org.uk/__data/assets/pdf_file/0006/671649/
    Letting_agencies_-_The_price_you_pay.pdf

26 http://england.shelter.org.uk/__data/assets/pdf_file/0007/624391/
    Rent_trap_v4.pdf

27 http://england.shelter.org.uk/_data/assets/pdf_file/0007/624391/
    Rent_trap_v4.pdf

28 http://www.bbc.co.uk/news/uk-england-london-20943576

29 http://www.bbc.co.uk/news/uk-england-london-20943576

30 http://england.shelter.org.uk/__data/assets/pdf_file/0007/624391/
    Rent_trap_v4.pdf

31 http://www.moneymarketing.co.uk/average-deposit-for-house-
    purchase-reaches-26500/1064230.article

32 http://england.shelter.org.uk/__data/assets/pdf_file/0006/671649/
    Letting_agencies_-_The_price_you_pay.pdf

33 https://www.gov.uk/government/uploads/system/uploads/attachment_
    data/file/284648/English_Housing_Survey_Headline_Report_2012-
    13.pdf

34 http://england.shelter.org.uk/__data/assets/pdf_file/0009/781587/
    Final_copy_of_Shelters_response_to_the_Government_Review_into_
    poor_conditions.pdf.

35 http://england.shelter.org.uk/__data/assets/pdf_
    file/0003/774093/2014_6430_04_9_Million_Renters_Policy_
    Report_Proof_6_opt.pdf

36 http://www.theguardian.com/housing-network/2014/jan/10/housing-benefit-under-25-young-people-cuts

37 http://www.theguardian.com/news/datablog/2014/jan/21/record-numbers-young-adults-living-with-parents

38 http://www.theguardian.com/housing-network/2014/jan/10/housing-benefit-under-25-young-people-cuts

39 http://www.mirror.co.uk/news/uk-news/richest-mp-britain-slams-welfare-3178089

40 http://www.mirror.co.uk/news/uk-news/richest-mp-britain-slams-welfare-3178089

Chapter 5

1 http://www.economicvoice.com/britains-household-debt-time-bomb/

2 http://www.economicvoice.com/britains-household-debt-time-bomb/

3 IPPR figures, cited http://www.telegraph.co.uk/news/politics/10539945/Recovery-built-on-housing-bubble-and-consumer-debt.html

4 http://www.bbc.co.uk/news/business-25152556

5 http://www.scribd.com/doc/206239093/The-State-of-Living-Standards

6 http://www.scribd.com/doc/206239093/The-State-of-Living-Standards

7 http://www.scribd.com/doc/206239093/The-State-of-Living-Standards

8 http://www.resolutionfoundation.org/press/debt2018/

9 https://www.moneyadviceservice.org.uk/files/indebted-lives-the-complexities-of-life-in-debt-november-2013-v3.pdf

10 https://www.moneyadviceservice.org.uk/files/indebted-lives-the-complexities-of-life-in-debt-november-2013-v3.pdf

11 https://www.moneyadviceservice.org.uk/files/indebted-lives-the-complexities-of-life-in-debt-november-2013-v3.pdf

12 https://www.moneyadviceservice.org.uk/files/indebted-lives-the-complexities-of-life-in-debt-november-2013-v3.pdf

13 http://www.stepchange.org/Portals/0/
    StepChangeLifeontheEdgereport.pdf

14 http://www.legalandgeneral.com/library/protection/sales-aid/
    W13612.pdf

15 www.parliament.uk/briefing-papers/SN06676.pdf

16 http://www.dailymail.co.uk/news/article-2706361/Payday-loan-firms-
    drove-Samanthas-dad-suicide-But-death-didnt-stop-hounding-him.
    html

17 http://www.publications.parliament.uk/pa/cm201314/cmselect/
    cmbis/789/78902.htm

18 http://www.publications.parliament.uk/pa/cm201314/cmselect/
    cmbis/789/789.pdf

19 http://www.publications.parliament.uk/pa/cm201314/cmselect/
    cmbis/789/789.pdf

20 https://www.gov.uk/cma-cases/payday-lending-market-investigation

21 http://www.stepchange.org/Portals/0/documents/media/reports/
    StepChange_Debt_Charity_briefing_on_unsolicted_marketing_of_
    payday_loans.pdf

22 http://www.stepchange.org/Mediacentre/Pressreleases/
    paydayloansnuisancecalls.aspx

23 http://about.brighton.ac.uk/sass/news/2013/130123-debt.php

24 http://www.stepchange.org/Portals/0/
    StepChangeLifeontheEdgereport.pdf

25 http://www.dailymail.co.uk/news/article-2706361/Payday-loan-firms-
    drove-Samanthas-dad-suicide-But-death-didnt-stop-hounding-him.
    html

26 http://about.brighton.ac.uk/sass/research/publications/Debt-and-
    Mental-Health-Report.pdf

27 http://www.dailymail.co.uk/news/article-2668999/Payday-giant-
    Wonga-fined-2-6million-sent-letters-FAKE-law-firms-scare-customers.
    html

28 http://about.brighton.ac.uk/sass/research/publications/Debt-and-
    Mental-Health-Report.pdf

29 http://webarchive.nationalarchives.gov.uk/20140402142426/http:// www.oft.gov.uk/shared_oft/consultations/OFT664Rev_Debt_ collection_g1.pdf

30 http://www.citizensadvice.org.uk/index/pressoffice/press_index/press_ office-newpage-20130903.htm

31 http://www.workingforwalthamstow.org.uk/fca-risks-legal-loan-sharks- slipping-through-their-net-says-mp/

Chapter 6

1 http://www.lv.com/assets/life/pdfs/press/coac-report.pdf

2 http://www.rbs.com/news/2014/03/calculate-the-cost-of-raising- children-with-natwest-app.html

3 http://www.lv.com/assets/life/pdfs/press/coac-report.pdf

4 http://www.dailymail.co.uk/news/article-2358836/The-cost-having- baby-Expectant-parents-need-5-500-bank-starting-family--wait-money. html

5 http://www.dailymail.co.uk/news/article-2358836/The-cost-having- baby-Expectant-parents-need-5-500-bank-starting-family--wait-money. html

6 Childcare Costs Survey 2014, http://www.familyandchildcaretrust.org

7 Childcare Costs Survey 2014, http://www.familyandchildcaretrust.org

8 http://www.politicshome.com/uk/article/95488/labour_childcare_ costs_put_off_7_in_10_mums_from_return_to_work.html

9 http://www.ons.gov.uk/ons/rel/elmr/gdp-and-the-labour-market/q1- 2014--may-gdp-update/sty-gdp-g7-economies.html

10 http://www.cpag.org.uk/child-poverty-facts-and-figures

11 http://www.cpag.org.uk/child-poverty-facts-and-figures

12 Childcare Costs Survey 2014, http://www.familyandchildcaretrust.org

13 Childcare Costs Survey 2014, http://www.familyandchildcaretrust.org

14 Childcare Costs Survey 2014, http://www.familyandchildcaretrust.org

15 http://www.familyandchildcaretrust.org/holiday-childcare-survey-2014

16 http://www.telegraph.co.uk/women/mother-tongue/10492109/IPPR-Governments-childcare-tax-relief-plans-are-regressive-and-wont-help-hard-working-families.html

17 http://www.telegraph.co.uk/women/mother-tongue/10492109/IPPR-Governments-childcare-tax-relief-plans-are-regressive-and-wont-help-hard-working-families.html

18 http://www.lv.com/assets/life/pdfs/press/coac-report.pdf

19 http://www.trusselltrust.org/resources/documents/foodbank/6323_Below_the_Breadline_web.pdf

20 http://www.lv.com/assets/life/pdfs/press/coac-report.pdf

21 http://www.telegraph.co.uk/finance/personalfinance/10385226/Pester-power-costs-parents-460-a-year.html

22 http://www.dailymail.co.uk/femail/article-2513702/Average-childs-Christmas-list-adds-nearly-900.html

23 http://www.theguardian.com/money/2014/jan/21/record-levels-young-adults-living-home-ons

24 Great Pay Robbery, www.tucg.org.uk

25 http://www.theguardian.com/money/2014/jan/21/record-levels-young-adults-living-home-ons

26 http://www.suttontrust.com/our-work/research/download/267

27 http://www.bbc.co.uk/news/education-26954901

28 http://www.theguardian.com/education/2014/jan/15/cost-cheapest-student-accommodation-rises

29 http://www.timeshighereducation.co.uk/news/student-part-time-work-increases/2006956.article

30 http://www.telegraph.co.uk/finance/personalfinance/10072716/Average-wedding-now-costs-more-than-18000.html

31 http://www.telegraph.co.uk/finance/personalfinance/10072716/Average-wedding-now-costs-more-than-18000.html

32 http://www.theguardian.com/uk-news/2014/jul/08/grandparents-stop-work-support-families-childcare-costs

33 http://www.theguardian.com/society/2014/mar/26/cuts-vulnerable-older-people-without-state-social-care

34 http://www.bbc.co.uk/news/uk-24424785

35 http://www.dailymail.co.uk/news/article-2406229/Care-home-bills-9-3-years-Average-annual-cost-room-28-367.html

36 http://www.bbc.co.uk/news/uk-england-sussex-24579496

Chapter 7

1 http://www.nao.org.uk/report/the-restructuring-of-british-energy/

2 http://www.Independent.co.uk/news/uk/politics/ios-investigation-the-great-british-energy-ripoff-8219565.html

3 DECC, Estimated impacts of energy and climatechange policies on energy prices and bills, March 2013

4 http://www.uswitch.com/media-centre/2014/05/consumers-owe-energy-suppliers-464-million/

5 http://www.publications.parliament.uk/pa/cm201314/cmselect/cmenergy/108/108.pdf

6 http://www.citizensadvice.org.uk/press_20131117

7 http://www.ukace.org/wp-content/uploads/2014/02/ACE-and-EBR-fact-file-2014-02-Fuel-Poverty-update-2014.pdf

8 http://www.parliament.uk/business/publications/research/briefing-papers/SN05115/fuel-poverty

9 https://www2.le.ac.uk/departments/law/research/cces/documents/the-energy-penalty-disability-and-fuel-poverty-pdf

10 Macmillian Cancer Support (2009), cited, https://www2.le.ac.uk/departments/law/research/cces/documents/the-energy-penalty-disability-and-fuel-poverty-pdf

11 http://bura.brunel.ac.uk/handle/2438/6832

12 http://www.europeanclimate.org/documents/LR_%20CbC_study.pdf

13 http://www.energybillrevolution.org/fuel-poverty/#section_winterdeaths

14 http://www.theguardian.com/money/2013/apr/20/energy-bills-prepay-meters-cost-poorer-households

15 http://www.dailyrecord.co.uk/news/scottish-news/cost-energy-rises-900000-sses-2801194

16 written evidence,7.5, http://www.publications.parliament.uk/pa/
cm201314/cmselect/cmenergy/108/108.pdf

17 http://www.publications.parliament.uk/pa/cm201314/cmselect/
cmenergy/108/108.pdf

18 http://www.telegraph.co.uk/finance/personalfinance/consumertips/
household-bills/9734447/E.On-raises-energy-prices-by-9pc.html

19 http://www.telegraph.co.uk/finance/personalfinance/consumertips/
household-bills/10692194/E.On-UK-energy-supply-profits-leap-26pc-
to-296m.html

20 http://www.nodashforgas.org.uk/why-we-must-stop-gas/

21 http://www.nao.org.uk/wp-content/uploads/2013/11/10286-001.
Full-Report1.pdf

22 http://www.mirror.co.uk/news/uk-news/centrica-fatcat-sam-laidlaw-
claims-3293434

23 http://www.theguardian.com/business/2012/mar/30/centrica-sam-
laidlaw-pay-bonuses

24 http://yougov.co.uk/news/2013/11/04/nationalise-energy-and-rail-
companies-say-public/

Chapter 8

1 http://actionforrail.org/new-public-ownership-calls-as-rail-fares-set-to-
rise-25-per-cent-since-2010/

2 http://www.justeconomics.co.uk/rmt-report/

3 http://www.tssa.org.uk/en/whats-new/news/index.cfm/it-s-official-
private-rail-firms-have-been-ripping-you-off-for-20-years

4 http://actionforrail.org/uk-commuters-pay-over-three-times-more-
than-most-european-passengers-2/

5 http://www.passengerfocus.org.uk/research/publications/national-rail-
passenger-survey-nrps-at-a-glance-great-britain-wide-spring-2014

6 https://www.gov.uk/government/uploads/system/uploads/
attachment_data/file/252516/rail-passengers-crowding-2012-revised.
pdf

7   http://www.yorkshirepost.co.uk/news/main-topics/general-news/
    chiefs-vow-to-raise-game-as-rail-survey-hits-out-at-overcrowding-1-
    6388094

8   http://orr.gov.uk/publications/reports/gb-rail-industry-financial-
    information-2012-13

9   http://www.transportforqualityoflife.com/u/files/120630_Rebuilding_
    Rail_Final_Report_print_version.pdf

10 http://www.theguardian.com/uk-news/2014/apr/16/rail-operators-
    200m-dividends-subsidy

11 https://www.gov.uk/government/uploads/system/uploads/
    attachment_data/file/4203/realising-the-potential-of-gb-rail-summary.
    pdf

12 http://www.publications.parliament.uk/pa/cm201213/cmselect/
    cmpubacc/813/81302.htm

13 https://fullfact.org/factchecks/do_train_operating_companies_earn_
    massive_profits-29273

14 http://www.telegraph.co.uk/finance/newsbysector/
    transport/10364459/East-Coast-Main-Line-returns-208m-to-taxpayer.
    html

15 http://www.transportforqualityoflife.com/u/files/120630_Rebuilding_
    Rail_Final_Report_print_version.pdf

16 http://www.transportforqualityoflife.com/u/files/120630_Rebuilding_
    Rail_Final_Report_print_version.pdf

17 http://www.ippr.org/news-and-media/press-releases/
    britain%E2%80%99s-buses-broken-by-deregulation

18 http://www.bettertransport.org.uk/sites/default/files/research-files/
    Buses_In_Crisis_Report_AW_PDF_09.12.13.pdf

19 http://webarchive.nationalarchives.gov.uk/+/http:/www.competition-
    commission.org.uk/inquiries/ref2010/localbus/pdf/00_sections_1_
    15.pdf

20 http://www.bettertransport.org.uk/sites/default/files/research-files/
    Buses_In_Crisis_Report_AW_PDF_09.12.13.pdf

21　http://www.bettertransport.org.uk/sites/default/files/research-files/
　　Buses_In_Crisis_Report_AW_PDF_09.12.13.pdf

22　http://www.bettertransport.org.uk/sites/default/files/research-files/
　　Buses_In_Crisis_Report_AW_PDF_09.12.13.pdf

23　http://www.ippr.org/publications/greasing-the-wheels-supporting-and-
　　improving-britain%27s-rail-and-bus-services"

24　http://www.ippr.org/publications/greasing-the-wheels-supporting-and-
　　improving-britain%27s-rail-and-bus-services

25　http://www.theguardian.com/uk/2010/jun/24/bus-operators-profits

26　http://valshawcross.com/val/wp-content/uploads/2014/01/140124-
　　Fair_Fares_-_London_Cost_of_Living_Report.pdf

27　http://valshawcross.com/val/wp-content/uploads/2014/01/140124-
　　Fair_Fares_-_London_Cost_of_Living_Report.pdf

Chapter 9

1　http://www.ons.gov.uk/ons/rel/social-trends-rd/social-trends/social-
　　trends-39/chapter-6.pdf

2　http://media.ofcom.org.uk/facts/

3　http://www.theguardian.com/money/2014/aug/28/bt-phone-and-
　　broadband-rivals-eye-transfer-market

4　http://media.ofcom.org.uk/facts/

5　http://www.parliament.uk/business/committees/committees-a-z/
　　commons-select/public-accounts-committee/news/rural-broadband-
　　report-publication/

6　http://www.ons.gov.uk/ons/dcp171778_322713.pdf

7　http://www.telegraph.co.uk/technology/internet/10010003/Lack-of-
　　understanding-keeps-half-of-older-people-offline.html

8　http://www.ons.gov.uk/ons/dcp171778_322713.pdf

9　http://www.bbc.co.uk/news/education-20899109

10　http://yougov.co.uk/news/2014/02/04/third-mobile-owning-teens-
　　also-own-tablet/

11　http://stakeholders.ofcom.org.uk/binaries/research/consumer-
　　experience/tce-13/cost_value_final.pdf

12 http://www.thisismoney.co.uk/money/bills/article-2127572/Mobile-phone-users-wrong-tariffs-wasting-5bn-year--study.html

13 http://www.citizensadvice.org.uk/index/pressoffice/press_index/press_20140314.htm

14 http://www.theguardian.com/politics/2014/aug/11/nationalise-mobile-phone-companies

15 http://www.theguardian.com/politics/2014/aug/11/nationalise-mobile-phone-companies

16 http://www.moneysavingexpert.com/news/phones/2013/02/kids-spent-3200-iphone-avoid-app-charge-hell

17 http://www.independent.co.uk/arts-entertainment/tv/news/outrage-over-commercialisation-plans-for-bbc-world-service-9039198.html

18 http://www.mirror.co.uk/news/uk-news/bbc-licence-fee-bargain---4081608

Chapter 10

1 http://www.realbritainindex.org/summary

2 http://www.nytimes.com/2006/11/26/business/yourmoney/26every.html?_r=0

3 http://budgetresponsibility.org.uk/economic-fiscal-outlook-december-2014/

4 http://www.realbritainindex.org

5 http://www.bbc.co.uk/news/uk-24424785

6 http://www.taxresearch.org.uk/Blog/2014/09/22/new-report-the-tax-gap-is-119-4-billion-and-rising/

Index

Action Groups

After reading this book one factor should come as no surprise. There is no shortage of campaigning groups, radical policy networks, and anti-austerity forces.

Boycott Workfare (http://boycottworkfare.org)
A UK-wide campaign to end forced unpaid work for people who receive welfare. Workfare profits the rich by providing free labour, whilst threatening the poor by taking away welfare rights if people refuse to work without a living wage.
Intern Aware (http://www.internaware.org.uk)
Campaigns for basic standards that would deliver fair internships for all.
Living Wage Foundation (http://www.livingwage.org.uk)
The Living Wage campaign was launched in 2001 by parents in East London, who were frustrated that working two minimum wage jobs left no time for family life.
Fast Food Rights/Hungry for Justice
(http://fastfoodrights.wordpress.com)
Campaign against low pay and zero hours contracts, and for trade union rights – in the fast food industry and beyond. The campaign links up with the inspiring global movement which has seen thousand of fast food workers in the US lead strikes against employers like McDonalds, securing a rise in the minimum wage to $15 across the city of Seattle.
Disabled People Against the Cuts (http://dpac.uk.net)
"Disabled people should not be the scapegoats for the financial mistakes of governments, should not be constantly told that there is no money to support them by millionaire politicians. We will not tolerate further erosion of our living conditions or our human rights, nor will we sit quietly while they try to take our rights away."
Citizens' Income Trust (http://citizensincome.org)
Promotes debate about the desirability and feasibility of a Citizens Income.

Radical Housing Network (http://radicalhousingnetwork.org)
London-based coalition of groups fighting for housing justice.

Fuel Poverty Action (http://fuelpovertyaction.org.uk)
Fuel Poverty Action campaigns against the injustice of cold homes by turning up the heat on rip-off energy companies and the politicians in their pockets.

Campaign against Climate Change/One Million Climate Jobs
(http://climate-change-jobs.org)
A campaign which received inspiration from action taken by the workers of the Vestas wind-turbine factory on the Isle of Wight, who occupied their factors when it was slated for closure.

Action for Rail (http://actionforrail.org)
A campaign which aims to work with passenger groups, rail campaigners and environmentalists to campaign against cuts to rail services and staffing and to promote the case for integrated, national rail under public ownership.

Campaign for Better Transport (http://bettertransport.org.uk)
"Transport affects everyone, so we never work alone: we support hundreds of local groups and individuals around the country, and bring together dozens of national organisations. Together, we campaign in a number of different ways for sustainable transport."

Campaign for Press and Broadcasting Freedom
(http://cpbf.org.uk)
Long-standing campaign for "a more accountable, freer and diverse media".

We Own it – Public Services for People Not Profit
(http://weownit.org.uk)
Aims "to shift the debate on public ownership, to show that public services are better in public hands. We want to help create a change in government policy. The people who use and pay for public services should come before private profit".

Reviews of
The Failed Experiment

"crucial exposé of neoliberal dogma,
crammed with fact and detail, making
it wonderful ammunition in the fight
for social justice."
Owen Jones, journalist, broadcaster
and author of *Chavs: the
demonisation of the working class*

"This book sets out to explain those economic concepts
and practices which most economists and commentators will
not deign to explain. Understanding these are vital if you do
not want to be helplessly buffeted about by mystical economic
forces. That's why it is a must-read."
Ann Pettifor, Director of Prime Economics and a fellow of the
New Economics Foundation

"Great analysis, strong politics and an inspiring call to arms."
John Hilary, Executive Director of War on Want and author of
The Poverty of Capitalism

"This is the best thing I have read in years. It will be readily used
by campaigners as a basic handbook to explain our recent history."
John McDonnell, Labour MP for Hayes & Harlington

"It wasn't hard to pick a political book of the year ... Andrew
Fisher's The Failed Experiment stood out for me."
Richard Murphy, author of *The Courageous State*

"Recommended for reading by all Red Labourites."
Red Labour